NO REDEMPTION

NO REDEMPTION

TAX LIEN AUCTIONS, EVICTIONS, AND LESSONS FROM THE FORECLOSURE CRISIS.

BY

TIMOTHY E. GRAY

NO REDEMPTION:
TAX LIEN AUCTIONS, EVICTIONS, AND LESSONS FROM THE FORECLOSURE CRISIS

Windy City Publishers
2118 Plum Grove Road, #349
Rolling Meadows, IL 60008

www.windycitypublishers.com

Published in the United States of America

ISBN#: 978-1-941478-20-2

Library of Congress Control Number:
2015956120

Windy City Publishers
Chicago

"Buy the ticket, take the ride"

~Dr. Hunter S. Thompson

In memory of David R. Gray

CONTENTS

DISCLAIMER

THIS BOOK IS the account of the last fifteen years of my life. My life has been mostly work, and I've documented every part of it. I have supported many of the stories with photographic documentation, because quite frankly they might be difficult to believe otherwise. But, believe if you can, as this is as honest a recollection as you'll ever read. In essence, history is mainly just that, a recollection; and I will admit that certain people in the book (especially the dishonest attorneys) may have a slightly different opinion and recollection. I get to use my First Amendment right to free speech, and I hold onto it with dear life, as these evil people are best at abusing the legal system to their benefit—hence this disclaimer. But for the others—the unfortunate ones we evicted, the lucky ones we helped, and the ones who rely on me to put food on the table: it is all a matter of perspective. That is all that matters, this is my perspective and this is my book. Whose version of history can be totally accurate, since it is all a matter of interpretation and remembrance? This is worrisome because in some cases I honestly mean no offense; but in others, I mean tremendous offense.

INTRODUCTION

MANY YEARS AGO, I started a company called Wheeler-Dealer, which became Wheeler Financial, which became one of the largest real estate tax lien firms in Cook County, Illinois. I am also an award-winning real estate broker and an auctioneer for real estate and charity events.

In the last fifteen years my company has invested over $125 million in tax lien certificates throughout the Chicago area, obtaining hundreds of tax deeds (equaling hundreds of evictions) when no redemption was made from the tax sale—including those of gang members, hoarders, sovereign citizens, drug addicts, squatters, celebrities, innocent renters, and the dead. I have dealt with many dreadful situations, such as evictions of disabled veterans, elderly widows, and the mentally ill. My company has rehabbed countless homes, at times taking terrible eyesores and restoring them to the community. I have been given hugs by tearful and appreciative neighbors when we evicted those who sell drugs on the block. We have worked with many subsidized housing programs for people facing homelessness and have seen their young families grow up in our rental properties through the years. As a company, we have even financed homes for families needing a second chance by creating a rent-to-own program for those who are unable to get traditional financing. We have both benefited and suffered from the results that come from each of the above. There are many lessons to be learned from our experiences, which in many cases we learned the hard way. But most importantly, I survived.

Survived at least, to this point. A slight shift in history over a few crucial moments in my life and the end may have been closer than I care to admit. For instance, there was a high impact collision that knocked me around the back of a taxicab like a pinball in an arcade game. Another time, it was an ugly lawsuit. And I can't forget the financial crisis; including tense moments with a lender, as suddenly they wanted to "exit the industry" and be repaid money I did not have. Can I expect more of those moments to come? Unfortunately, yes. Perseverance, I remember thinking, is what separates achievers from those who fail. If you can survive the night and wait long enough, night eventually turns to day. Well, I waited. And waited. And I have to say, the night is long. But it can change in a flash. I eventually left the hospital. I won the lawsuit. I found another bank to replace the tense lender. In this book, you get a taste of everything: from best to worst, an all-you-can-eat (if you will) offering from the tax lien buffet.

As entertaining as these stories are, it is not the stories of the people that have driven me to write this book. Rather my focus is on the homes themselves and what we can learn from them. A brick home built in 1934 has seen many families move in and out over the years. In most cases, many mortgages have been placed on it, perhaps a tax lien or estate sale, maybe vandalism that gutted the entire building, or fire damage that was eventually restored. Perhaps the neighborhood went from blue collar to white collar over the generations, and the home that once housed an immigrant janitor (like my grandfather) now houses a millionaire stockbroker. Same house. Same bricks. Same land. A home that was over mortgaged in 2006 and became a boarded up foreclosure the next year did nothing wrong. While I have found in many cases the people involved are great people, great people can make terrible decisions. And a savvy investor can profit from those bad decisions. Now it will be the same house on the same land in 2026 as it was in 2006—only the value and the condition fluctuate, and both are controlled by us.

I attended my first auction when I was a teenager and was instantly hooked. I became an auctioneer for several reasons, but one was I wanted to understand how an auction works. If you have ever been to an auction, you may have seen someone get a great deal on an item and wish you had placed a bid; conversely you may have seen a bidding war between two large egos that resulted in real buyer's remorse for the winner. So how do we discern between the two, and how can one prevent the latter from happening? I have an entire chapter devoted to auctions and buying strategies and the secrets I've learned (here's a sneak peak: the real winner of an auction comes later, when the winning bidder resells the item, not immediately after the auction). Of course, you need not attend an auction to be part of the bidding process; you may find yourself making an offer on a property that has a "multiple offer situation" and essentially become part of a live auction without realizing it.

Let's step back a few years to the late 1990s. I was a film major in college, and upon graduating, landed various gigs in the entertainment industry. A few were fun and somewhat profitable, but for the most part it was one disaster after another. No one hears about or even considers the number of movies that get produced but never released, and I was part of an awful one that changed the course of my life for good.

The movie, set in Florida, was cast with a former wrestling star and one of Hollywood's elite actresses from the 1950s. Also set to co-star was a chimpanzee, who we were told could be taught almost any trick, from shooting pool to riding shotgun in a motorcycle through the lush Florida trails. It was to be directed by a 1970s industry heavyweight who hadn't make anything watchable in over 25 years. Some ideas are better left—ideas. Besides a poor script and terrible directing, there was an awful production director who would have made a better warden at a penitentiary. She was technically an attractive woman, but at times I had my doubts if she even had human DNA. And then there was me—young, dumb, and ready to assist in any way possible. So dumb in fact that midway through production when the weekly paychecks stopped coming in I actually believed her when she claimed I would get paid that following Friday. Of course, on that following Friday, I heard (and believed) the very same story. On that third (or maybe fourth) Friday, it was very clear I was working for free, as was the rest of production department. Soon after, many of the employees were let go, and I was among the first sent packing.

I'd never been happier or, unfortunately, more broke. Somewhere on the bottom of the worlds "cutting room floor" this film was laid to rest—mercifully. For a few years after I admit to being bitter about it: a total waste of my time enduring the long twelve-plus hour days. Time is money after all; I wasted time and received little money for my effort. At some point years later it occurred to me that real people lost real money on this endeavor, an amount that must have totaled millions. I wasn't worried about them at the time of course; I was more concerned about the eviction notice on my door.

Unlike tax liens, the entertainment industry is very risky. While the rewards can be great, the odds for success are low. The probability is even lower when you create a terrible product. Not everything turns out well in life, and the important thing is to move on having learned some lessons from your past, and hopefully become wiser in the future. My lesson in this dismal experience was the importance of having a contract, a document in which I later found great solace. Looking back on it, I think even the chimpanzee had a contract. Real estate transactions are most always secured by enforceable contracts, including what commissions will be paid and to whom, what the purchase price is, the amount of earnest money, and a host of other details many other industries seem to avoid. This became my favorite part of buying and selling real estate, and I still go off-the-chain when someone signs an agreement and tries to rescind or change the deal. Being honorable and trustworthy is by far more important than any profit, and a reputation is all you have. While we live in a seemingly large world, it is a round world and everything does actually (and literally) spin around in circles. I am tortured with an excellent memory, but even if I was not, we all seem to remember those who betrayed us, lied to us, or left a negative impact. You may receive a thousand compliments to one insult, but it is the insult that you never forget, isn't it?

And insult you they do at almost every turn. You must be tough to survive in the tax lien industry, because you deal with constant adversity. For instance, you need to fight to be awarded the tax lien. There are usually many bidders at the tax sale, and while some are cordial, some are just miserable people. Some liens are miserable investments too—properties in need of total repair. If you find you are the only one bidding on the property, there is probably a good reason why. The best properties attract multiple bidders, and it can be very competitive just to be awarded the tax lien. From that point, you have a homeowner that may not take kindly to your new investment that is secured by their home. Of course, if you ask the court for a tax deed there might be a mortgage company or heir that may object. If you do get issued the tax deed, an eviction is always stressful and often adversarial. And if all of that isn't enough, whomever you sell the home to is likely to be a handful: asking for a survey, garage door clicker, tax prorations, and lawn care— none of which you have or will agree to. The entire process is a headache.

So, this book has many uses, in some ways this book is based in sociology, in others it is instructional. In some cases, comedy, and where there is comedy lies tragedy. Unlike others to come before me, I make no assertions about "getting rich quick," nor do I think that is even possible, other than playing the lottery. I do not purport to have any specific formula for making money in real estate, but within these writings are some excellent points and strategies about how to become successful in the real estate industry. Organization and good business principles are the keys to my success—simple fundamentals that have not changed in generations. In this fast paced world we live in, it is more important than ever to go back to basics, and in my case, to reflect on what I've accomplished, hoping others will benefit from the honest words I've written.

THE 1999 SCAVENGER SALE

I T ALL BEGAN when I attended the 1999 Cook County scavenger sale. This is a tax sale held once every two years for properties that did not sell at the annual tax sale—basically the worst of the very worst. The scavenger sale was a rare occurrence, designed to erase up to twenty straight years of tax delinquency with a mere $250 minimum bid. The counties in Illinois, especially Cook, have a very tight budget and great need to collect property tax. Should a homeowner fail to pay their property tax for any given year, the county treasurer will sell that receivable in the form of a tax lien. The homeowner has approximately two-and-a-half to three years to pay it off with interest, or as the winning bidder, you can petition the court for title to the home. Across the United States tax lien sales have become a billion dollar industry. The more a county needs its uncollected property tax money, the more they need tax sales. Cook County is no exception. Instead of collecting from each individual delinquent home-owner, the treasurer simply conducts a tax sale and brings in the vast majority of unpaid money within just a few days. The properties that do not sell at the tax sale will try their luck again at the scavenger sale. The quality of the properties in the scavenger sale generally ranges from bad to worse. My late father joked that the biggest insult I could give a homeowner is *not* to bid on their home at the tax sale. I agree; if a home is not sold at the tax sale, then it must be awful. And if it is truly awful, then it belongs in the scavenger sale. If you pay the minimum bid of $250 and wait the statutory amount of time one of two things *could* happen. Similar to the annual tax sale, you could get paid back your investment plus interest if the homeowner redeems the tax lien; or you could take title to the property if there has been no redemption. These are the best-case scenarios, overly simplified to help explain the complicated structure. You *could* also lose your money.

The process seemed fair to me, if you fail to pay your personal income tax you can lose your freedom and be jailed for the offense, so it stands to reason that if you fail to pay your property tax you can lose your home. At the very least, high interest penalties would be assessed in both scenarios. In the case of the scavenger sale, these were the properties no tax buyer wanted at the annual tax sale, so the homeowner has no urgency to pay the bill since there is no collection effort being enforced. Years would go by and the tax would begin to add up, so the treasurer found a handy way of resolving this: by offering it to so-called "scavengers" like me. But, unlike me, the group of scavengers includes a host of unscrupulous other characters—the real scavengers, as you'll find out.

I must admit, the idea of wiping out twenty years of unpaid property tax for only $250 sounded too good to be true, similar to those late-night infomercials about buying an expensive suburban home at a tax sale for pennies on the dollar. Like those same infomercials, there is *always* more to the story; technically it may be partially correct, but in reality it couldn't be farther from the truth.

Not all states in America even have tax sales; Wisconsin for example does not allow it. But for the states like Illinois that do, it is a tremendously efficient method to collect unpaid property tax amounts. For instance, the Cook County annual sale usually recovers approximately $50 million in cash over the course of only four days, from companies like mine fronting the money to the county on behalf of people who failed to pay on time. Giving the homeowner almost three full years to pay it back with interest and penalties is incredibly fair, but as we all know, time does fly when one is having fun and not paying tax.

Getting back to my first tax sale in 1999, the process was not automated in any way, and for approximately six weeks, eight hours a day, I sat there and listened to an incredibly bored and possibly tortured auctioneer reading off each individual parcel number, one by one, to see if anyone was willing (or dumb enough) to bid the minimum $250 on the property. When someone did place a bid the auctioneer seemed a bit shocked, possibly aggravated to interrupt the cadence of reading number after number, over and over again. Some auctioneers grouped the numbers up for speed, saying "Double-o eight," but some others preferred the slower "Zero zero eight" to call the number. Each Parcel Identification Number (PIN) is sixteen digits long, and they only read the number not the address. An example might be 20-14-202-008-0000. The last four digits notate a home over a condominium; if the number ends -0000 it means it is not part of a condominium. Some auctioneers actually read out loud, "Twenty, fourteen, two zero two, zero zero eight, zero zero zero zero. Are they any bids?" If not they said, in the most monotone and sad way possible, "Offered, not sold." If there was a bid on the item, the minimum was $250 and then the bidding began and went up from there until the highest bidder was found and awarded the tax lien. Quite often there were spectators, the same crowd who saw those late night infomercials and believed this was the way out of their regular job. The issue they immediately found is that to the naked eye, or ear, there is absolutely no way to identify what is going on or what they were bidding on. There were no photos of the property, and each bidder must do such a tremendous amount of research prior to the tax sale that it quickly became a part-time job. The problem is most of the people were there to avoid working another job; the infomercial apparently didn't mention needing to do actual work or researching dusty tax books in the county library. Most of the infomercials, books, and seminars written on the subject of tax sales are very poor. The authors have never made a living buying tax liens. They may know the industry in theory, but a theory does not help you profit from your investment dollars. They can't warn you of the pitfalls because they have no clue what they are. If you were sick and needed complicated surgery: would you turn to a doctor who has researched the operation only in theory? Or would you choose the doctor who has the most amount of surgical experience? There is no handbook for instruction on how to buy and sell tax liens. Most of the tax buyers won't share their secrets; as they don't want the added competition in the room.

A few years later, one amateur investor got an idea to follow me out of the tax sale room at lunch, and when I sat down at a restaurant to eat, he sat next to me without asking permission. "Wow, this is really exciting," he said. "It is?" I replied. He went on and on about how interested he was in buying tax liens, but he admitted to having no knowledge how to go about it. To his credit he had heard of the many pitfalls that await people like him and wanted some advice from me to avoid losing his investment. I wasn't going to talk specifics, but he seemed genuine, so I suggested he know exactly what he was bidding on before actually placing a bid. I told him to learn as much as he could over the next year and then attend another tax sale when he was a bit more educated. "But I could just see this being a great way to invest!" He wasn't taking no for an answer, and so I quickly finished eating and politely said goodbye. Before leaving, he said, "I'm going to do it today! I am going to do it!" Less than thirty minutes later he bought two liens, and was incredibly excited as he dashed out of the room to pay for his new purchases. He never returned, but I did note the two liens he purchased. One was polluted marshland; the other was a landlocked sliver of useless land.

On another occasion, the auctioneer was reading hundreds of numbers in an area of no active bidding. Two Federal Marshalls walked in and grabbed a bidder who seemed to expect what was coming, as he made no effort to resist and didn't seem surprised. The auctioneer, not missing a beat declared: "Twenty, fourteen, two-o-two, double-o-four?— Offered, not sold. Double-o-five? Offered, not sold. Bidder Number 19 has been taken into custody. Double-o-six?"

At this point you may be wondering why I kept showing up in the tax sale room after that first auction in 1999. The answer is quite simple, I was learning. Occasionally a good lien was found deep within those dusty old tax books.

It was probably one in every few thousand, but if you look hard enough at every oyster, occasionally you'll find a pearl. I quickly graduated from the scavenger sale to the more prestigious annual tax sale. For the most part my first few years consisted of buying only vacant lots in Chicago. I did this because they were cheap; many lots have less than $500 per year in taxes. The very small amount of capital I had was deployed at somewhat high interest rates, since only the interest rate is the subject of the bidding at the annual tax sale. The county just wants the money it is owed, therefore, the only question is what interest rate is placed on the homeowner redeeming the property. Most liens are sold at 0 percent interest, another aspect that is often overlooked in the many books and infomercials on the subject. While many believe tax liens are a good investment, a 0 percent return on your money is hardly a good use of your investment dollars.

In the case of building my business, I was able to identify a plan of success that no others had considered. This was in the form of vacant land, which I had gotten to know quite well from my hours spent researching the scavenger sale in 1999. There was little to no competition for these lots, since most of them are fairly close to worthless, and other tax buyers seemed more interested in bidding on homes and large commercial properties, which at the time I could not afford. I bought as many of those lots at the highest rates I could, and to my delight, many of them did in fact redeem. My competition thought I was nuts, and when my brother took a day off from law school to come watch me bid someone said to him, "Your brother is buying half of the west side. What is he thinking?" Well, I was able to make a handsome profit from the owners of those lots who redeemed their taxes.

There were many that had "no redemption," as it's called, and I quickly became the owner; with no real plan to liquidate them. I realized I needed a real estate license in order to sell them to the public, so I obtained one. By using an incredible marketing tool known as the Multiple Listing Service, as well as at auction, I offered them for sale. Timing is always an important factor, and because I bought these lots in the year 2000 and needed to allow almost three years before I could own any of them, I found myself selling in 2003 when home building was extremely popular. In addition, financing was plentiful for home builders, especially in high-risk areas. Because times change and real estate is fickle, these very same lots are now close to worthless, perhaps worth less than $500, but at the time they were selling from anywhere from $15,000 to almost $230,000 for one large tract of land at Seventy-Ninth Street and Loomis Boulevard in Chicago. This was purchased by a developer who obtained approval from the local alderman to construct a community of town homes, yet today it still sits vacant, exactly in the same condition with the very same dirt as when I sold it over a decade ago. The land did not change at all; it was simply the demand that dictated its price—and that's what made it a good investment for me. On the settlement statement at closing was a personal note to me written by my brother who was then a newly licensed attorney, which simply read, "Nice one!"

This was the start of what was to be an incredibly wild ride in the tax lien business. Not all liens are profitable, which is why it is important to have the ability to absorb mistakes. These are government-conducted sales, and they are serious business. Quite honestly, I caution against anyone going into the tax lien industry. I have seen too many investors lose money or buy poor quality liens. Though I offer instruction to help minimize the risks, they can't be ignored. Tax liens are usually sold over the course of only a few days. Since they are all purchased at the same time, they all expire on the same date. All of the notices must be sent on the same day, and if you miss a deadline you don't just lose out on one of the tax lien certificates—you lose on every single lien in the portfolio. Although the underlying collateral is considered low risk, tax liens require expert servicing, and if not serviced properly the money used to purchase them becomes very much at risk. Rather, I suggest developing personal relationships with tax buying firms, as most have an existing inventory of real estate they are always looking to liquidate. Many of the larger tax lien firms are backed by large private equity companies and not interested or equipped to handle individual real estate. Their purpose is to invest money, while most tax lien investors are only looking for a small and manageable portfolio or income producing real estate. There is a time-value component at stake as well. Why wait three years when you can buy something today? As an investor, you risk much less buying from them directly than going to a tax sale having little knowledge of local laws and policies.

I have seen tax buyers sent to federal prison, many totally wiped out financially, and others just embarrassed at the tax sale for their lack of knowledge. Should you be the one to actually ask a question at the tax sale, the entire room will erupt with loud laughter at your expense. This is a team effort to humiliate you into never returning. And it works. While some teachers advise there are no dumb questions, in the world of government auctions, there is no such thing as an intelligent question. You either know what you are doing or not, and any sign of weakness will be used against you. It is very similar to the animal kingdom, with the exception that animals are much better behaved than my competition of tax buyers, who are mostly ferocious, greedy, and looking to profit at your expense. One amateur tax buyer managed to buy a small but nice portfolio before running out of money (and time) to service it properly; and subsequently the competition picked away at his portfolio until he had nothing left. He was unable to continue paying the property taxes as they became due, which is necessary to secure the tax lien. Most of the competition took delight in his failure—and I suspect they did so to prove a point. With a three-year redemption period, as an investor you need patience and the ability to finish the race.

At times, I marvel at how I've navigated the rough waters, and I was "a small fish in a sea full of sharks." Now, years later, I am a big fish, and I am changing the industry by acting with compassion, transparency, and the work ethic of a thousand men. Part of my passion stems from the amount of distain I have for some of my competition, the way the old ghouls have treated me, and the way they treat homeowners on the verge of eviction. They take pleasure in it like cruel sadists, and whether they know it or not, they have helped me become bigger, more profitable, and most importantly, more loved within the community than all of them combined. This is because I care. When you are down and out, possibly facing eviction, or trying to relocate your family and get a fresh start after a job loss, some kindness and compassion are most welcome—yet rarely available. If you had to have your home sold for taxes, far and away, you are better off having my company purchase the lien. We do more payment plans, counseling, workouts, and optional delinquency notices (which look like bright orange parking tickets) than anyone else.

While most tax buyers want a person's home for profit, we often just want redemption, as we get paid the money owed with interest (if any) and the homeowner keeps their home. It is only after all attempts have failed that we conduct an eviction, including in some cases offering cash for keys and providing a list of local agencies that help work with those facing homelessness. As you are about to read, once it gets to the eviction stage, it passes the point of no return and becomes personal—there is no going back. Generally I have no compassion dealing with someone's investment property where they collect rent but do not pay their taxes, but the owner-occupied homes, especially those occupied by the elderly or the disabled, do get our fullest attention and compassion. Should I finance a property I already own to someone who fails to pay, or rent to someone who refuses not only to pay but to even answer the phone, it becomes open season. 90 percent of the time I am a very easygoing, compassionate person. But, there's this other 10 percent, and if someone wants to play, hardball is my favorite sport.

TAX DEEDS AND LITIGATION

I F NO REDEMPTION has been made from the tax sale after approximately three years, you, as holder of the tax lien, may petition the court to issue a tax deed. This is provided you have strictly complied with the provisions of the property tax code. If you do not, or if you've made any mistake, you could lose your entire investment.

For example, say the property is located at 6913 S. Main Street, but the homeowner doesn't like the number 13, they may use 6915 S. Main Street for no other reason than superstition. However, as a tax lien purchaser, if you use the wrong address on any one of your legal notices, the judge likely will deny your application for a tax deed. It is that simple. The last recorded deed and assessor will say the address is 6913, but the owner changed it to 6915. He can prove that with a simple photo of his address sign and utility bill. What are you supposed to do? The answer is not simple. If you pursue a court battle, it can be costly, especially if you do not have a brother who is a top attorney. You may, and likely will, win the case if you used 6913, but it will cost you, cutting into your profit substantially. One answer is to use 6913-15 S. Main Street.

One of the most head scratching situations I've experienced was a six-unit apartment building we attempted to obtain a tax deed on in Des Plaines, Illinois. The building was converted from an apartment building to condos. The owner did not pay that last year of tax that was owed when it was an apartment building and converted it to condos, probably in an attempt to not pay tax, and sell each unit for quick cash. These conversions were popular during the real estate boom when condos were highly sought after and the rental market was very weak. We put all six of the unit numbers on the legally required notices we sent out. However, we encountered a problem: all of them did not fit in the space provided. These notices must be in strict compliance with the law, so there can be no changes in formatting.

So we bought a tax lien on an apartment building that suddenly turned into six individual condos. Those individual unit owners were served notices for real estate taxes on an apartment building—but how could that be when they just bought an individual condo? They didn't feel like paying those funds, and no redemption was made from the tax sale. We asked the judge to issue a tax deed. There was a mortgage company involved who later admitted in court they simply missed the payment date and had planned to redeem the tax sale in time but failed to do so. They were hoping the former owner would redeem the taxes of approximately $31,000— but why should he? He had sold all six condos and cashed out. The bank that provided the mortgages to the new owners hired an attorney who argued our notice did not strictly comply with the Illinois property tax code, which stated that the address on all legal notices must be in at least ten-point type. Of course, using ten-point type would not enable us to fit all of the unit numbers on the notices. In the end, the judge sided with the bank, saying the notices were defective and did not strictly comply with the property tax code. So we lost out on a nice profit, and I left the courthouse wondering how I should have handled that admittedly rare situation. If I had left off one of the unit numbers to make the address fit in ten-point type then the notice would surely be defective, but if I included them all they simply would not fit in the small space allowed on the notice. Most of the time we successfully defend our proceedings against litigation, which is a large part of this business. Unfortunately some rare cases like this do occur. You'll need to budget plenty of money for legal fees when buying tax liens.

I remember obtaining a tax deed to a parking lot used and owned by a national pharmacy, one of the largest pharmacies in the world. You would think they were flat broke when it came time to settle the tax deed matter. First of all, they owed the tax. It was the pharmacy drive-thru and parking lot. They made plenty of profit literally selling drugs at a drive-thru window to pay their property tax. But they did not pay, and we obtained a tax deed. They admitted the mistake, and an attorney from the company called me to discuss the matter. He was a very nice, older, mellow, kill-you-with-kindness gentleman who said, "You have less than $10,000 invested in this lot, right? How about we give you $15,000 and that gives you a 150 percent return on your investment, which is tremendous by anyone's standards." And while he had a good point, I noticed on my last inspection that the drive-thru was backed up with cars looking to buy legal drugs. It is important to inspect and document everything and have photos time stamped as well on every inspection. We save every photo by the PIN, so we can easily search years' worth of photos on a drive and have proof of the condition sorted by date. We had to litigate for years over the matter, because they were too cheap to make any type of reasonable settlement offer. Eventually they realized the gravity of the situation, so when we settled the case, I had already bought police tape and was ready to drape it all over the lot. It was hard to convince the sheriff to evict only the drive thru and parking lot area of a pharmacy, but I was trying my best.

Whether it is a bank or a pharmacy, it never ceases to amaze me how some people procrastinate. I remember one time an employee of a company was directed to redeem our tax sale before she went on maternity leave. When she returned a few months later, she discovered we owned the land. That had to be a tough conversation with her boss, and I can only assume she no longer works for that company. They eventually purchased the land back from us, but insisted they would only enter into a new contract to purchase it. Even though they had already owned the land, for accounting and publicity reasons, they wanted it to appear as if they were purchasing new land as opposed to settling litigation. I am sure they were all applauded for such a wonderful new real estate acquisition, but they all should have been terminated for incompetence. This is not a random occurrence. Recently, an employee of a real estate developer failed to redeem a tax sale on a parking space in a building they constructed. She confessed that she knew the date but simply missed it. She was shaken; worried it might cost her employment at the company. She asked for a price. It wasn't easy telling her the amount. I am sure it was harder for her to hear it. To her credit, she paid the amount from her personal savings account. I admire her ability to take responsibility, and the respect she had for her employer.

There was a condominium in Chicago right off Lake Michigan to which we obtained a tax deed. This was a very nice townhome-style unit on Sheridan Road. It was previously bank owned and was listed by a realtor as a foreclosure. It was for sale when we received the tax deed. I noticed on her listing the unit number was the same as ours, but the PIN did not match what we had purchased at the tax sale—and the PIN is really the only thing that matters. When asked about the discrepancy, the realtor who sounded like a heavy smoker said in a raspy tone. "I don't check the PINs, hon." So we obtained a tax deed to the condominium, and she couldn't have cared less about this error, feeling no remorse for her client, and deflecting blame for her negligence. I have no proof of this, but I feel the bank had the wrong PIN entered into its system, and so when the notice we sent was received they likely checked their computer system for the PIN, did not get a match, and discarded the notice. They assumed they did not own the property. When no redemption was made, we obtained a tax deed, having served the bank, and they had no defense. I believe there were many levels to this negligence; the employee from the bank made no effort to ask why they were sent that delinquent tax notice and the realtor who's very job it is to list the unit accurately simply did not care. This was an outstanding sale for us, yet admittedly a rare situation. You can't count on the incompetence of others to make a living, but it sure is nice when it happens.

Quite often we obtain tax deeds to investment properties occupied by innocent renters. The owners, knowing full well they are behind on the property taxes, often fail to mention this to their unsuspecting tenants. Some have no intention of redeeming the tax sale, but rather, they keep collecting and depositing as much rent as possible while paying out as little as possible until the day finally arrives they no longer own it. I have seen investors purchase homes at foreclosure sales for less than $25,000, and after cheaply repairing the property, rent it for up to $1,250 per month over the course of the three-year redemption period, depositing almost $45,000 in rental income. Property tax per year on such a home may be $3,500 or more, cutting into their profit drastically if paid.

Recently we received a tax deed to a condo in a large, middle class, condominium complex. The former owner set up a company to purchase the condominium from a bank, paid less than $12,000 for the property and never paid a single installment of tax or condominium assessments. Of course, he had rented the unit until the condo board began their collection efforts. Being an expert at evading service, and never showing up at the actual property, the condominium association found it very hard to serve him the legal notice to demand their money. Soon after, his company folded like a lawn chair, essentially shielding him and creating another layer of confusion, all the while the renter continued paying him rent. The cost of the taxes after three years outweighed his own purchase price, and by the time we obtained a deed some three years later, the condominium association had obtained a forcible entry order to take possession of the unit for back assessments and obtain the rental income. This method, although profitable for him, is simply disgraceful.

The Circuit Court of Cook County is often referred to as the Circus Court of Cook County, as there is a type of magic, run by a new generation of clowns and trapeze artist who roam the hallways on every floor. They know every trick in the book to delay the inevitable and spin their creditors around in circles. The court system, disturbingly set up for leniency on behalf of the deadbeat homeowner or renter, allows this manipulation to occur. For example, even with a solid case against a renter who does not pay you, it could take up to one year to evict the person. It takes months to get proper service, even though the eviction paper is referred to as a "five-day notice." If they do not pay on the sixth day you may file your case. But you have to serve the person with a legally required notice, and they take elaborate steps to avoid being served. Of course, the easiest thing to obtain in Cook County is a continuance. Most will ask for time to obtain legal counsel, but of course, upon the next court hearing there has usually been no appearance filed by any attorney, as that would cost real money. If you should be so lucky to serve them the legal notice yourself, they will likely deny it ever happened, so you must have the judge appoint a special process server, a fee you won't recoup, or get it on video. If the process server should serve the required notice, often the judge will stay an order for possession for up to ninety days, and only at that time can you tender the order to the sheriff; but the sheriff in Cook County is more overwhelmed than the court system, and it could take two to three additional months to evict. You had better hope it does not snow on the day of eviction, rain heavily, or occur during their holiday moratorium when the sheriff does not evict anyone for almost the entire month of December. If so, you go right back to the bottom of the line, and have the privilege of waiting an additional three months. I have seen a sheriff refuse an eviction on a condominium we own because the unit door itself did not have the unit number posted on it. The sheriff would not take my word for it—how would I know what unit it is, after all I am only the owner? To the back of the line I went, and now we keep a variety of letters and numbers on hand and affix them to the unit doors on the morning of the eviction. The only thing missing at the landlord-tenant floor of the court house are the circus lights, the announcers, the music, the elephants—all of which I see and hear in my head when having to deal with these clowns. Instead of garbage cans they should place rodeo barrels in the courtroom to complete the desired circus effect.

There was one instance when I obtained a deed to a property and decided to rent it out. It was a three-unit building, but one of the tenants lied on his application and purported to be employed at an auto body shop. I called to verify employment, not realizing I was simply talking to his friend who confirmed his fake employment. I asked for first and last months rent, which was paid, but unfortunately that was the last money I ever received. He was truly a nightmare tenant, and I took it quite personally. He wouldn't answer the door or respond to my calls. I posted a forty-eight–hour notice to enter the premises and conduct a safety inspection. On the forty-eighth–hour, he would not answer the door so we drilled through the locks, assuming there must be some emergency, perhaps a leaking gas line or failing smoke detector that needed attention. Of course, I am always entitled a "wellness visit." It was my building after all, and that was my right with the required time in advance. When we entered he was cowered in the corner, amazed I could be so brash, but standing right behind me was the court appointed special process server who placed the legal notice in his hands to pay all of the rent he had owed plus late-fees within five days. When he showed up to court, he claimed we illegally entered the premises and when the judge disagreed, the tenant then called me a racist. (As if a racist would rent to him in the first place, and also ignoring that the other two families in the building were a different race than me and loved me.) The judge had only one question for him, "Did you pay him or not?" You could almost see his brain working and a dimly lit light bulb go off above his head when he declared, "YES! I paid him in cash and received no receipt!" He asked for time to produce a witness who was present when he allegedly paid the fraction of the amount he had owed (my policy is once a person is far behind, I *only* to accept the full amount; partial payments are never accepted). The judge gave him two more weeks, but the witness's testimony quickly fell apart when my brother asked him under oath to describe the apartment. To my amazement, the witness who was not expecting such a question declared he could not describe the apartment, (he had clearly never been inside of it) because he had been drinking heavily at that time. The judge, to his credit, had heard enough, but all told it took months to evict him. The tenant and the witness both should have been arrested on the spot for perjury. Of course, this was never considered. We had developed enough disdain for each other by then to make the Cold War seem friendly, and he did all he could to destroy the apartment before the eviction. By placing the first and last months rent, totaling a mere $1,600, he was able to secure the apartment for over one year, by simply learning the ways to manipulate the court.

The vast majority of judges in Cook County are excellent, but the forum in which they must work is very flawed. If ever there was an industry in need of a total makeover from the top to the bottom, it is the legal profession. I have seen both defendants and their attorneys and some plaintiffs' attorneys lie to the court and the judge—the law somehow allows the plaintiffs complaint to be taken as the truth, even if there is no truth to any of the writings. At one point I had proof that two attorneys (from different firms working together in an failed attempt to obtain money from me) had lied in their replies to my defense—literally lied in writing and they knew it. I went to my own attorneys inquiring about making an Attorney Registration and Disciplinary Commission (ARDC) complaint—the organization in charge of policing the industry, ironically made up mostly of lawyers. My attorneys' response from them was frightening: "If the ARDC would sanction every attorney who lied, and investigate every complaint of dishonesty, there may be very few attorneys left." No truer words have ever been spoken, and eventually the two dishonest attorneys I had to deal with lost their attempt to get paid a single penny from me, but at the expense of my attorney fees, which did not get reimbursed.

Litigation cannot be avoided, because if you become successful, there is a tremendous amount of jealousy on the part of your competition and others who see you as an open checkbook. Once I dated a woman who owned a well-known live music venue in Chicago. I was struck by the alarming number of law suits they endured almost weekly: those who sued because they fell (while drunk) or got into a fight (while drunk) and were injured when the bouncers removed them; or even a father who sued when his underage daughter came home drunk, when it was her own fake ID that procured the alcohol. Because of these baseless claims, and the fact that none of these people accepted any responsibility for their own actions, the insurance expenses on that night club were astronomical, as well as their yearly attorney fees. Some high-risk companies even have their own attorneys on full time staff, dedicated only to fighting off senseless litigation. The only answer to these convoluted situations is a total reconstruction of the legal system: holding plaintiffs responsible for the attorney fees once they lose and making dishonesty an offense punishable by loss of an attorney's legal license.

There are complicated financial systems as well. The funds I use to purchase the tax liens are somewhat highly leveraged and not easy to obtain. My progression of borrowing funds through my career went up and down depending on my financial statements, the economy, and the ability to conform to the banks covenants. These covenants are basically guidelines that you must follow at all times. Should you violate even one covenant you will be in default, and the bank may call the loan. If not, you will surely be subject to a covenant violation fee, which only makes these guidelines harder to follow.

At one point I was required by a bank (whom I no longer do business with) to obtain a $10 million life insurance policy, which was actually written in my loan agreement. I was only able to qualify for a portion of that at a cost of several hundred dollars per month—written by the very same banks life insurance salesman. About twelve months later he called, asking if I was still alive, and if so, did I want to shop around and reduce my premium? I answered in the affirmative, and he sold me like a prostitute to every insurance company in the northern hemisphere, enclosing proof I had stayed alive for one full year since signing my last policy (I later learned this was important). He did reduce my premium, but I still took a pay cut every month for a policy that I won't be around to enjoy when it pays off.

I got into playing the life insurance game for a little while, hearing what the actuaries say about my life and health. They place premiums, basically wagers, on when you will die. If you owe the bank a lot of money financing your business, as I did, this money can be used to pay them off or make them feel easy lending you that highly leveraged money. After all, I was borrowing millions of dollars at the time, and it was going up. Yes, if I did die suddenly there should be a plan. But I live in Chicago and work in real estate, mostly on the West and South Sides—what could possibly go wrong? Did the actuary notice I have done hundreds of forceful evictions? I answered all questions honestly, as I always do, and even supplied a ton of financial information to prove I wasn't in financial turmoil. The actuary just seemed to care if I was into skydiving and possibly scuba. Was I planning on traveling abroad and do I enjoy the occasional smoke? A thrill seeker and smoker, I am not. Everyone would agree, doing forceful evictions in the most dangerous city in the world is much more risky than scuba or skydiving. But that's why I have Big Mike.

EVICTIONS

BIG MIKE ISN'T actually referred to as Big Mike in real life, but often I refer to him as Big Mike because to me, Mike is plenty big. When I have needed property management or bodyguard protection service, he, along with Big Heavy, keep me safe. Big Heavy makes Mike look small, in the way I must look compared to Mike. But Mike is much more than that; he is a close friend first and foremost, but he is also a carpenter, a firefighter (not literally he puts out all of my fires), an eviction specialist, a locksmith, a property investor in his own right, family man, and overall badass.

We met around 2004 when he was rehabbing a town-home attached to the townhome I had just received a tax deed on. Mine was vacant and I had the sheriff do the eviction. They drew their guns; I loved it. I asked if I could kick the door open. They told me to back off, and used this torpedo looking device to force the door open and send pieces into oblivion. They took immense pleasure in this; even if you had the keys, it was a race to fumble with them before they ram the door with the torpedo. Mike and I met that day, and we exchanged numbers. I had a few crews that did my rehab work—we would fix the door the sheriff destroyed and correct any dangerous condition. Paint and carpet can go a long way.

Mike called occasionally, asking me if I had any work to be done. He must have had a good feeling I was onto something special because he kept calling, saying, "Hey, Tim. It's Mike. Just calling to bother you again." And I loved it; I loved the willingness to be part of my team. I thought, let's give him a home, and see what happens. Right from the top our partnership was easy. The first home was a "hot mess" as he would say, and he took care of like it was nothing. It was amazing. I had no headache at all. He was both the good cop and bad cop; he could be incredibly sweet and compassionate, but if someone was disrespectful, it was game-on: hardball. And that was my favorite sport too. I thought, welcome aboard Mike. Honesty and loyalty have been his calling card, and that's all that matters to me. If he had overpriced me on those first few homes like everyone else did, or found something wrong that actually wasn't wrong (I've actually caught someone making up a problem that did not exist) it would eventually catch up and cost him work in the future. No one knows what the future holds, and in Mike's case the future was going to be bright because he was tenacious and then conducted a professional honest operation.

If you follow-up, offer your talents, do honest "Good Business," as we call it, you increase your chances of success exponentially—I cannot stress this principle enough. In the rare event you do fail, people will respect you because of your honest business principles, and you will be known as a lady or gentleman when you depart. I have ended business relationships many times, but always with a handshake and look in the eye.

You must take your own professionalism seriously, if you borrow money you must treat it as your money; but it isn't your money—that's why you borrowed it. You do not own anything you've financed until you've fully paid it off. If you have a mortgage, someone else owns your home. When someone calls you telling you to refinance, it is only because they will profit from the refinance, not because they actually want to save you money. Pay everything off as quickly as possible if you need to borrow funds. Remember, you can always pay *over* the amount owed, but you can never pay *under*. During the hard times, you'll need to be sure you can make those monthly payments. The banks love you in debt—especially in default—often making it worse by charging penalties if you are struggling, which only make your struggles worse because, well, you are struggling. I highly suggest only spending money you have and borrowing money only to purchase assets that will increase in value.

Back to Big Mike: we have done over ten years of evictions together, sometimes with him flying solo, others with me and the help of my German shepherd, Roxy. Mike and I have had a few very dangerous evictions, and occasionally it gets very heated. While we always try to diffuse the situation, sometimes it cannot be controlled. I remember one occupant causing a lot of trouble both during and after the eviction: threatening me, throwing things at my car, disturbing my sleep. I had given him my cell phone number to arrange to move his belongings, but he would call in the middle of the night, drunk and threatening me. I called Mike late at night, venting to him, and his response was simply: "No, no, no, I'll take care of this, Tim. This is personal now." I am fortunate to have been accepted within the toughest communities. One time a young man got in my face as I was taking over a boarded up home on my own. His boss told him to back off, saying, "Leave him alone. No one else is going to do anything with this place." We turned that home around, and that is good for everyone in the community.

Evictions are never easy. My very first eviction was a profound learning experience, which took place in a suburb about thirty miles south of Chicago in a subdivision of Markham, Illinois, known as Coral Gables. This subdivision was the antithesis of the affluent Miami subdivision known by the same name—it had small concrete shacks and broken down cars in the driveway instead of sprawling homes and yachts. One of every three homes was vacant and boarded up, and this particular home was occupied by an alarming number of angry people. The eviction was set to go down anywhere between 8 a.m. and 2 p.m., which is a large time frame to sit out in front of someone's home. The occupants didn't like seeing me reading in my car and called the local police. When the police arrived, I had assumed they were the ones who would conduct the eviction. It had not occurred to me at the time that the Cook County sheriff would be showing up a few moments later to do that job. The local Markham police asked what I was doing there, and I showed them the court order, and said, "OK, let's do this." They explained they had been called because of me; shocked I said, "You mean, you are not here to evict them?" They had a look of fright when they realized what was about to happen. Here they have a guy sitting in a Pontiac Grand Am who is about to forcefully remove the very same occupants who called them for help. The policeman, after checking with his supervisor, asked me to wait halfway down the block until the sheriff arrived.

At that very moment, two Cook County sheriff squad cars and one beat-up older junk car came racing down the block. These were clearly the guys; they parked on the curb, they were completely in control. Along with the local police, about half of the neighbors watching, and the occupants, two sets of sheriffs officers pulled their guns and immediately took control of the building, forcing everyone out and then raiding the home checking for guns and drugs or anything else illegal or dangerous. In the old junk car sat about four plain clothes mean looking guys whom I later learned were on work-release programs from Cook County jail, their job was to physically move out all of the possessions into the street (a practice which stopped a few years ago due to liability issues and theft). This crew was pretty backed up and had a lot of evictions to cover that day (or wanted to go to lunch) as they really only carried a few large items out of the home. When they tired, the sheriff gave me the "no trespassing" sign and said to place it on the door. If anyone were to go inside without permission they would come back and arrest them.

I got slightly frantic, and said, "Wait, you are not leaving—are you?" The response was unexpected, the big Irish looking cop poked me in the chest several times, and told me, "You are in charge here; this is your place. You are the boss—remember that!" And they left as fast as they'd arrived. So did the local police. I was on my own dealing with these very angry occupants whom had already called the police on me. To my credit, I listened to the advice, and started screaming, telling everyone to listen up and go inside to get their stuff and get out. I secured the property with a metal hasp, removing all of the locks and using padlocks with combinations. I left and came back twenty minutes later, they were tossing rocks through the window, so I called the same local police that were called on me only an hour before. Everyone scattered, and I realized these are highly contentious situations. While it would be about two years before I met Big Mike, I knew I needed a self-defense class, a German shepherd, and a host of help.

A few weeks later that same Pontiac broke down in Robbins, Illinois, on a cold day. It attracted the attention of a few of the local kids who didn't feel like attending school. I remember trying frantically to use the key and start the engine while praying and hearing things like, "What's the matter white boy, your car break down? Your car ain't running? Did your car break down?" I was pretty sure I was in serious trouble, but instead I learned another valuable lesson. Two lessons actually: the first being I needed a new car, but more importantly, I learned they were not taunting me, they were genuinely asking me if I needed help with my broken down car. I called a tow truck, and we hung out and shared some laughs while I was waiting. I will admit they may have sold a fair amount of drugs while I was waiting that hour for the tow truck, but they were very friendly and nice. I never did see that car again; I bought a more reliable Acura that next day. I told the salesman I refused to go get the old car, and he sent someone to pick it up on the other side of town. Within a few years GM announced they would shut down their Pontiac division, which did not come as a surprise.

Shortly before I met Mike, I obtained a tax deed and subsequently had an eviction in the Little Village neighborhood of Chicago, a very ornate Latino neighborhood with great architecture and good property values. The sheriff came and cleared out the people, but they literally moved right back in. They clipped the combination locks with lock cutters and actually changed the locks. They posted a sign that said "stay out" in both English and Spanish. I had a Spanish-speaking crew at the time that was doing some clean outs and evictions for me, but they were at a bit of a loss. The Chicago Police Department was not very helpful, as they would come and clear the home, but the next day we had the same problem. Being crafty, we devised a plan. At the time, the home construction industry was doing well, and at every Home Depot I noticed many workers eagerly looking for work in the parking lot. Early in the morning anyone looking for fairly cheap labor would pick up workers and in the evening drop them off after paying them in cash (this is a practice I have not seen in years). We hired about twenty of those workers and basically stormed the building and took control of it. We used the safety in numbers principle, and it worked. I paid a few tough guys some money to stay there at night, and then quickly found a buyer and closed on it.

I obtained a tax deed to a home on Spaulding Avenue in the same neighborhood; I was working with the crew to repair the building. At the time I was obsessed with doing a lot of the work myself, but since running a business was a full time commitment, I could only stop by after working in the office and help out until 9 or 10 in the evening. I walked into a fog of heavy pot smoke that evening and barked, "Donde esta, Jorge?" Someone responded, but I had no idea what was being barked back to me, as what I'd said was the only Spanish I knew. I began helping to remove some old tiles in the main room. It was the middle of summer and the days were long: it was dusk when a tall off-duty looking police officer walked in, saying nothing but flashing some type of badge. My initial thought was he was going to bust these guys for smoking weed, but rather he walked into the bedroom, removed a loose tile and walked out with a bag of money. He casually left without saying a word. My first reaction was of amazement, and then disappointment; had I worked in that room I may have removed that tile myself. Later I surmised: Could this have been a drug dealer's home, and while sitting in jail he finally confessed to where the money was? I could only hope it was used as evidence in a plea bargain and not a vacation fund for the finder. It also explained the dense marijuana smoke; the workers had stumbled upon it during the construction and were not bashful in helping themselves.

At a gas station on Chicago's South Side, a former owner threatened to set the property on fire. He was still operating the business, refusing to vacate until the sheriff evicted him. We deployed security around the clock; armed security officers took shifts and watched the place until both the eviction and closing were completed. No fire ever occurred but twenty-four-hour security is very expensive. On another occasion, someone was breaking into a twelve unit building, and I hired an off duty police officer to conduct surveillance in an attempt to stop the theft. He was very confident he could do just that, and on that very first night he caught them in the act and roughed them up enough to prevent them from returning. He reported back that my problem was solved, and he didn't feel he needed to work at the site anymore; and you know what, he was right.

One of the most haunting evictions I did was without the sheriff, since this home on Park Avenue in Harvey, Illinois, appeared by all accounts to be vacant. The law allows me to take possession of a property myself once a tax deed is issued if the home is abandoned and vacant; this, as I found out, is risky. For starters there was no power, gas, or running water and the front door was boarded but hanging off the wall. I was inside to secure the building and take photos so I could list the property the next day. I can remember this very vividly; in the darkest corner of the home was an old recliner pointed toward the wall. Next to the chair was a bucket, which I discovered was full of the vilest liquid I had ever seen. A mix of vomit, urine, and feces. It was almost bubbling, obviously still warm, steaming from the cold conditions in the home. At that moment, I realized there was someone sitting in that chair, facing the corner of the room, inches from me. The chair swiveled around slowly to reveal a person, pale and weak. I am honestly unsure if it was a man or a woman. We locked eyes and I was frozen with fright. We said nothing; we just looked at each other. I wanted to say, "You'll need to leave," but instead I was the one who left. I backed out of the room slowly, as the chair swiveled back facing the corner.

Once Mike and I started working together, those stressors in my life decreased. He was able to handle all of these situations without me getting directly involved; and on the occasions when I was there and all riled up, he handled the conflict and was excellent at relaxing me. One time the sheriff refused to evict and I went off the wall. I was really riled up, and felt the sheriff was being lazy, looking for any excuse to move on and not evict. I was reading them the riot act, but Mike calmly repeated to me, "Tim, Tim. Calm down, Tim. Take a deep breath, now. Come on, Tim." It was excellent advice; you can never win in that situation. Often we take turns playing a good cop–bad cop of our own. One time we walked through a totally gutted and dangerous twenty-four-unit apartment building, which was a tax lien that did not redeem. This was a hot mess, totally trashed and unsafe, yet when we purchased the tax lien three years before it was really nice and well occupied. A very inquisitive yet foul smelling neighbor came at me asking questions—and because of his intoxication, did not realize how close he was standing to me or how aggressive he came off. This did not go over well with Mike, who stiff-armed the guy sending him flying backwards saying, "Whoa, whoa, back off the boss." The man did just that and immediately left the scene, his questions unanswered.

Mike helped with an issue on Superior Street on the city's West Side. This was a former owner who would not work with us. He was insistent he would never leave the house. I know this because he told me many times, "I will never leave this house." So, unfortunately, we had to have him arrested, but he was released and moved right back into the house, as promised. This repeated itself on many occasions, he would get arrested and then break right back in. He would only move into the basement every time, not the main floor or second floor. He was a nice older man, never violent, but there was something about that basement, perhaps a comfort that he did not want to let go of. We had never experienced this, usually people get the hint, and if not the reality sinks in when they are in Cook County Jail, a place that is not for the faint of heart. Just the smell of Cook County Jail is a deterrent enough to avoid criminal behavior. One security guard we heard about got four months paid leave after a rat crawled up his leg and bit him. Crawled up his pant leg! If you notice, most guards tuck their pant leg into their boots and if you've ever wondered why, now you know.

Speaking of crime and punishment, we performed an eviction in Berwyn, Illinois. While it looked like a well-conditioned two-unit building, we did not know that a drug lord previously owned it and that the authorities had totally ransacked the home after the arrest. There were no floors—literally the floor was earth, they removed everything, only dirt remained. It was cavernous and was a total loss. From the outside, it looked like a lovely home, but on the inside it was a reminder of the risks of buying a home sight unseen.

I recently did an eviction on the West Side of Chicago. They refused my cash for keys offer, and would not answer any mail. I checked the day before hoping they may have moved out prior to the pending eviction. But unfortunately, they were very much still there. It was probably 2:00 p.m. when I arrived and the party was in full swing. I could hear loud music from down the block. The house was packed with people. On the front porch people were drinking, smoking, and dancing. I couldn't believe my eyes. They were literally waving their hands in the air, and yet, they were being evicted the very next day. In a way I was envious; not only did it look like a fun party, but also this is the greatest example of living in the moment I have ever seen. The next morning—everyone was gone.

Most of the time the sheriff schedules the evictions based on proximity, which is a smart decision for efficiency. They assign certain crews to certain areas, and your waiting time depends on where your eviction is located and the number of evictions pending in that area. For instance, we did an eviction two years ago in Palatine, a semi-affluent northwest suburb that only took three weeks. We received a tax deed, and I had met with the owners in their home to work-up a payment plan so they could avoid the eviction. I really tried to work with them, but the occupants were incredibly mean and lived in filthy conditions with stains on everything and unruly kids screaming. They were cooperative at first, but then refused to pay even a single month of rent. When confronted later about the nonpayment, his wife became belligerent telling me to "go back to my mansion." There is a common misconception about wealth in this business. Most of the time, the margin is tight. Not all liens are profitable, especially when the bidding is at 0% interest. I have a nice home in Chicago, but a mansion it isn't. I had recently broken up with my girlfriend who also lived in Palatine, so I think in some ways I transferred my hurt forward onto them once they disrespected me. Like a good journalist, I try not to become part of the story. In this case, I took it very personally. Just being in Palatine was difficult enough, and this woman was calling me every offensive name in the book. I felt like I was being roasted.

When the sheriff showed up a few weeks later, it got ugly. It was one of the few mornings I was excited to get up early. Immediately, she started calling him all sorts of blasphemous names, and I realized it wasn't personally about me. She does that to everyone, although I seemed to get it the worst. The sheriff took a much better approach to her abuse than I did, and calmly repeated her insults back to her. (Oh, you think I'm a pig?) I promptly sold the home; and not sure I've ever returned to Palatine.

For an eviction in the town of Ford Heights, Illinois, a small, poor community known for its proximity to the Ford Motor plant, it could take the full twelve weeks. We had submitted three homes for eviction, all of which were up on the same day. The sheriff, when they are ready, will only call the day before the eviction. These three were up and all went down without an issue. They were vacant and got the full attention of the neighborhood, which is very quiet during the day and very rowdy at night. We passed out some business cards and left the area. Within a few days I received many calls from neighbors wanting to buy the homes, but I didn't feel safe going back there alone to sell them. I called Mike and asked him to bring Big Heavy along; we would do a tour of all three homes and attempt to sell them in one day, a modified open house of sorts. I felt like I was famous: Big Heavy made sure no one was in each house and then would escort me inside while Mike stood outside to wrangle the onlookers. The first home sold quick for $10,000 and the buyer whom I've come to know and respect a lot, had $2,000 in cash as earnest money. Big Heavy saw him take the cash out and noticed we were in the main room. He grabbed me and led me into a bedroom with no windows, fearing we would be shot if anyone saw that amount of money. We signed the contract, I took the money, gave him a receipt, shook hands, and off to the second home we went. We met an older sweet couple in the next home, they wanted it for their daughter, but they clearly didn't trust anyone, including me. I was able to comfort their fears by telling them I was more nervous than they were. Pointing to Big Heavy, I said, "That's why I brought security." Big Heavy had a black sweatshirt with white bold letters that read, "SECURITY." The woman acknowledged, saying, "I can see that." And we sold that second home for $12,000. By the time we arrived at the third home the word had gotten out, there must have been more than fifty people waiting for us. After clearing the building we let people go in for ten minutes while Big Heavy and I stayed in the car. Mike identified three serious buyers; one of them was a young savvy well-spoken investor who purchased it for $9,000. These, of course, are typical prices for used cars not homes; they were all good deals for the buyers and for me. I drove home that day having sold $31,000 worth of property for approximately a $20,000 profit.

THE GOOD

B Y NOW YOU have to be wondering where the good is in this business. But what goes down must go up. We evicted a "house of porn"—it literally had X-rated photos on every inch of every wall, movies and catalogs piled to the ceiling, and numbers of strippers with notes describing their services filling the dressers. He was a combination of hoarder and sex addict. The neighbors were grateful; they endured a living nightmare for many years. I never met him; he knew the eviction was coming and on some level was too embarrassed by the interior condition to ever show his face again. We had to clean it out, loading a dumpster up with the pornographic images. The garbage company must have been in shock when that dumpster arrived: 30 yards of porn. Personally, I would have burned the entire dumpster. We used a company that recycled everything, but I am not sure these materials should even be recycled. When we were done, and it was thoroughly sterilized, you would never know it was a house of porn. Paint, carpet and, a primer called Kilz does wonders at times like this. We sold it to a new owner and though I was unsure of his porn habits, I am sure he was a better neighbor than the former owner was.

Another apartment building on Chicago's Northwest Side was very nice with the exception of the basement that had been converted into a small apartment. It was dark, dingy, and as it turned out, illegal. (I prefer to use the term nonconforming.) At the time we acquired the deed to the property, there was someone living in the basement, as well as the other two units. Because the basement was rented when I got the deed, I was unaware at the time that it was not to be occupied; but the basement always concerned me since I couldn't imagine anyone living there. When the occupant moved out within a few months, I placed it for rent for only a few hundred per month. I did the showings myself, and when one prospective tenant walked through the unit, I was expecting her to tell me how awful it was and how no one would ever want to live there. What I was not expecting was for her to proclaim, "It's perfect!" *Perfect*, I thought? *Has the definition of perfect changed?* The lesson I learned is that every place is a step up for someone; you cannot take for granted where someone has been living, if anywhere at all. She was just happy to avoid living where she was. When she moved out, we gutted the basement unit, turning it back to a simple common area to reduce my liability and conform to the city's building code.

After the basement was refinished, the tenant on the second floor of that building had asked me to check their furnace, so we walked downstairs together. It turned out to be an easy fix. As I left, his daughter was playing in the yard and there was a rabbit sitting there beside her. It was no ordinary rabbit; this looked like the Easter Bunny. It was well fed with big floppy ears and round eyes. Besides, it was entirely too clean and white to be living on the streets of Chicago, so I asked, "Whose bunny is this?" The father got defensive very fast, shaking his head saying, " I don't know; I've never seen it before." I wasn't buying that for a moment, so I looked at his daughter and asked, "Is this your bunny rabbit?" I find children to be much more honest than adults, and she quickly pled guilty by picking up and hugging the bunny, who seemed to be hugging her back, both thinking I would separate them. As it turned out, I didn't care (other than being lied to), but they feared I would get mad or terminate their lease; so when I arrived she took the rabbit and ran down the back stairs to the yard.

Sometimes a family I'm working with has become an extension of my family—that's the best feeling. There was one family who I had originally offered a unit for only $600 per month. The father said he traveled but needed a place for his wife and kids to stay. He guaranteed I would get paid from his job as a driver, and he did pay me for a few months; but then sadly, he was arrested for attempted murder. There were three kids, each one cuter than the next; the youngest was really shy. All of the children were so nice, and the mother spoke very little English. The oldest was only about seven when we met, and I was instantly amazed at how mature this young seven year old was as she translated for her mother; she seemed to understand things seven year olds are incapable of understanding. What seven year old worries about rent money, or explains to her mom she needs to pay it to avoid being evicted? But even though the woman didn't pay, I couldn't bring myself to do anything about it. I wrote off each month as they went by, and unlike the clown mentioned earlier who lied to me and didn't pay, this was different. This family needed help and deserved it. I sometimes came over and spent time with them, but then other times I needed rent money and was irritated. Those times the daughter was amazing in understanding and translating my semi-anger to her mom for hardly paying what she owed. "She says she understands and is sorry," she would translate back to me. It broke my heart. We put her in touch with a rental subsidy program called the Spanish Coalition for Housing, and she set up an appointment. The caseworker met the children and spoke with me at length, and they agreed to allow this family to become part of their program, which pays a vast majority of the rent.

Soon after, the Spanish Coalition for Housing merged with the Chicago Trust Fund, an organization run by the city that approves the unit for rent, not the tenant. Usually in Section 8 housing, the tenant will get a voucher, which they can take anywhere it is accepted and move in. When they move out, they take the voucher with them. But the Trust Fund approved the unit itself, so if the tenant should ever move, the fund would simply find another family that would reside in the unit. Of course, the city had very strict requirements to become approved, including a long background search, multiple property inspections to be sure it conformed to city code (the unit did not initially pass, forcing me to make expensive repairs). They even checked all of the other property we owned to be sure there were no outstanding violations on those buildings. All told, it was a financial disaster and paperwork nightmare, but one of the most rewarding experiences of my life. To watch these kids grow up healthy, in a safe, nice apartment is truly an American dream.

The next story is a lesson in tuning lemons into lemonade. We obtained a tax deed on two condos in the Ashland Towers complex on the South Side of Chicago. The unit numbers were 3I and 4I, one directly above the other. The same person owned both units at one point but then failed to pay the taxes on either one. He had intimidated everyone in the building and was very aggressive to his neighbors, and myself. To make matters worse, he knew just enough about carpentry to be dangerous, having removed the ceiling of the lower unit and the floor of the unit above to create a duplex. He took two electrical service meters and merged them into one service, making it very hard to restore the properties. But worse yet, he took the doors with him—including the front doors of both units that needed to be special ordered. It was the only eviction we have ever done when the sheriff just walked right in. (They were bummed they could not use the torpedo.) Of course, the former owner came back wanting to collect some of his tools, but by then we had installed two new doors with locks. He called me and was very angry, calling me a "punk" and demanding his tools. The condo board President called me to warn me of his abusive ways, and to be careful in dealing with him. He was dishonest and accused me on many occasions of stealing. He had run up a huge assessment bill, but thankfully the law does not require we pay for unpaid assessments before we owned it. A court ordered tax deed removes all imperfections of title and is essentially the best type of deed you can obtain. Although we were successful in removing him and his possessions, he ruined both units. Imagine one unit having a large hole in the ceiling and the other having a large hole in the floor. This was an item that needed immediate repair; I couldn't imagine anyone buying the unit in as-is condition.

But this home on the other hand, is just fine as-is.

The property taxes on the home above were sold in the tax sale, and we were the winning bidder. This is an example of what a tax lien seminar instructor might show you, to get you to imagine to possibilities of buying this stunning mansion for pennies on the dollar. Ah, wouldn't that be so nice. But with a stunning home, comes a stunning tax bill, which when added up over the course of four years (three years of delinquent taxes, one year to perfect title and gain possession) is a hefty sum of money. While there is certain equity in those figures, the fact remains, its nothing more than a dream. In this case, the homeowner redeemed the property at the last minute. Because the lien was so desirable, it did not attract a high interest rate, but was still a very solid, safe investment. It was a win-win either way. We profit from interest, or we take title and move into this beautiful home. The chances, however, that no redemption will be made on a home like this was very low. The lottery may yield a higher winning percentage than the odds of a tax deed being issued in this case. In the meantime, the money is not liquid. You can't force the homeowner to redeem even though you know very well he will. The homeowner knew the deadline and refinanced the home, possibly using the tax lien as leverage to modify a mortgage. With that much money at risk, the mortgage company does actually call you back. Large tax liens should generally be purchased with caution, but this is an exception to that rule.

Sometimes however, the conditions people live in are filthy. Some of my photos depict scenes that are unimaginable. It's one part of the job I have never quite adjusted to. For one, I hate roaches. Any bugs really; ants, spiders, and bed bugs are all particularly disturbing. But, nothing is more disturbing than a maggot infestation. Microscopic parasites such as scabies can be a nightmare, even if you do not have them. You just need to *think* you may have them. Even more frightening, very rarely is there just one roach. There are usually many roaches. No one gets just one scabby; they get full blown scabies. To avoid this you'll need to wear protective clothing. We have performed clean outs in full HAZMAT suits, which is particularly concerning for the neighbors to see. Some rotted food items are simply unidentifiable. There was one house in particular that smelled like rotted everything. You could not be inside of it without getting physically sick. We used industrial chemical respirator masks, but they were ineffective. After the clean out, we left the windows open in the house, hoping some fresh air might help. Neighbors from as far as two blocks away called the city to complain. I went back a few days later and they were right; that entire neighborhood smelled like that rancid house. Not knowing what else to do, I shut the windows and locked the doors—but not nearly fast enough to avoid becoming physically sick. The neighbors came outside to check on me; I must have sounded as if I was being tortured. I knew that closing the windows would only make the problem worse. It was a temporary solution to a gigantic problem. But everyone was complaining to me, as if I was the one who caused this. I had lost the support of the community, yet I was simply the sucker/successful bidder at the tax sale. From the outside, it was a beautiful brick single family home. I had no idea an environmental disaster was waiting for me. Even though the tax sale was the catalyst for this much-needed change, my role was to complete the transition. Often times this can be the hardest part, and you'll need a strong stomach. In this case, I did complete the transition and sold to someone who demolished the building as fast as the permit was issued. A new home was built on the land, resulting in another good outcome when there has been no redemption.

There was a home in Country Club Hills, Illinois, that was occupied, but the water service had been shut off—curiously they had a large fish tank in the living room. Even though the name of the Village is County Club Hills, not much of the area resembles anything you would find around a country club. I'll admit there are a handful of homes that are incredibly nice, but mostly it is a modest community. We conducted the eviction. We safely rescued the fish but how does one top off the fish tank with water or do water changes without water service? How does one even go to the bathroom without water? Once we evicted and found a buyer, we needed to do a village inspection; a process in which the building inspector walks through the property and points out various items that need to be repaired. When the building inspector showed up, he actually had the nerve to say, "You need to stop buying homes in this area." We laughed, he seemingly believed having boarded-up vacant homes and those occupied with no running water is better than having families who will care for the property and pay their water and tax bills. Every home we own is a home that was behind at least three years in property tax. They should be thanking us for returning it to the tax rolls, where the village obtains the revenue to use for schools, libraries, and yes, the building inspectors own salary. But sometimes logic is simply too much to ask. Tax buyers have a reputation (often well deserved) of being crooked, greedy, and unethical. I have worked very hard to change this perception, and though it won't be truly removed until the old ghouls are gone, progress is being made. Still, the reputation clearly carries on; and it may affect your investment. Besides prejudiced inspectors there are banks that will not lend in this industry. There are even first time homebuyers who are skittish about tax deeds, making it harder to resell when they realize their potential new home was a part of a court ordered sale. They'll assume you are an evil tax buyer who evicts elderly women on Christmas Eve simply for holiday entertainment. I don't have to look far around the tax sale room to see why these stereotypes exist; many of my competitors have earned the opinion so many have of them. As this generation of tax buyers changes hands, a new more compassionate one emerges. This is very promising for the tax lien industry, because when the time comes to say goodbye, there may not be a wet eye in the house.

Another similar home in Chicago had no running water but did have Comcast cable service in every room of the home. As I learned, the city of Chicago water department is much less tolerant of nonpayment than Comcast. When the sheriff walked in they laughed, showed me the TVs, took out the remotes and scrolled through a few channels as if they couldn't believe their eyes. I have seen sheriffs deputies make fun of those who own BMW and Lexus cars but do not pay their property taxes—and even worse get evicted. But the sheriff officers and I were all shocked that a person can live with no water service but had the essential utility of ESPN.

Among the most profitable liens we purchased was for two condominium units in high-rise buildings in downtown Chicago. The first was owned by a married couple that lived in the building; they had invested in an additional unit at the beginning of the foreclosure crisis, and had planned to rent it out. I believe they rented it successfully for a short time but eventually the couple fell on hard times of their own. They were able to continue to pay their bills on their principle residence but failed to pay the property taxes on the investment unit. This was a nice building, and this unit was on the twenty-fourth floor with a stunning view of downtown. The assessments in the building were approximately $550 per month or more, and when you add in property tax of approximately $10,000 per year, it simply became overwhelming. Although this condo did not have a mortgage on it, the tax and assessment alone was almost as much as the monthly rental income they received. This is certainly something most people fail to consider when purchasing an investment property, especially in a condominium building. When you add up the property tax and assessments, you basically have no room left to pay a mortgage. Even if the numbers work, it does not take more than a few months of a renter not paying you to create serious financial stress. Should they fall on hard times, you will need to pay those amounts regardless of whether the rental income is deposited or not. Should you get a renter who knows the ways of the Circus Court, then forget it—game over. In this case, the couple let it go to us when no redemption was made from the tax sale. To their credit, they held no hard feelings and left the unit in very clean condition. It sold very quickly; it was not listed for longer than thirty days. Since I had a tremendous amount of equity in the condominium I had the ability to price it very competitively.

The other unit was located on La Salle Street in Chicago, a very nice condominium building with a tainted past. The developer had some financial problems (to say the least) and had sold many of the units to unqualified buyers and the vast majority went into foreclosure. The unit we purchased at the tax sale had a large mortgage on it, and we served the mortgage company with the required notice. They did not redeem within the statutory timeframe, but they did file somewhat ridiculous objections to our tax deed proceedings. Subsequently we had to endure over a year of litigation before we could proceed and obtain possession of the unit. As I write, I am unsure if this story belongs in this chapter, or in the chapter called "The Unbelievable," because of what comes next. Since we profited handsomely from this unit I felt it should be included here, so let's call it a tie. Because of the litigation with the bank, the condo accrued unpaid assessments month after month. Eventually we won in court and I was able to obtain a key to the unit, which we assumed was vacant since the mail had been returned and the bank themselves had not rented it out (nor are they set up to be landlords). Imagine my surprise when I took the elevator up to the thirty-fourth floor and opened the door to find two half naked people lying in bed on a Tuesday afternoon. I can only describe them as "high end squatters" as they had absolutely no reason to be occupying this unit. They had no lease agreement, but did have fake suntans and resembled cast members of a reality show. They were both young and attractive but in a fake way, including their lifestyle which wasn't based in any type of reality at all. The man seemed angry and confrontational when I walked in; a big, dumb jock type. The woman was busy calming him down and asking me questions like: "Who are you?" "I'm the owner! Who the fuck are you?" I responded angrily, recalling my instructions during the Markham eviction years before. They went into the bedroom to get dressed, and we calmly sat down in their living room to discuss this strange situation. This building was very well secure, with access prohibited without a key fob. Immediately I knew the fix was in and demanded they come clean. I showed them a copy of the deed (issued one year before due to the litigation) and asked to see some type of lease agreement, which they could not provide. The man tried to speak, lowering the tone of his voice to try to appear more intelligent, but only made it worse as he was unable to explain how they obtained access to the unit: his story making no sense. Finally, the woman came clean: The building manager knew the unit was vacant and was pocketing a reduced rental amount while they were there. She told me they had lived in over six units in the building, including the penthouse for more than eight months, until someone would claim ownership of the unit and they would quickly move. "So, you are squatters, basically?" She was trying to add a positive spin, "Well, we are taking care of the unit. We moved in and no one said anything to us—we figured this unit was abandoned, no one has shown up for more than nine months." I explained the absence was because of the litigation, which was now resolved. We did not have possession, I said, but if they wanted to avoid an eviction and possibly being arrested for trespassing they needed to move ASAP. I also felt I had a claim against the property manager and company, so when I left I promptly banged on his door the same way the police might prior to a drug raid. The building manager previously had given us a bill for over $30,000 which we disputed since we are only legally responsible for assessments since the date of ownership. (Banks are notorious for not paying assessments.) But we did legally owe one year of assessments, which was not paid since we were unsure of the outcome of the litigation. I demanded any money they collected from these high-end squatters be applied to the balance or I would sue for fraud. He complied, was apologetic, and stated he was only trying to offset the unpaid assessment bill, which made even less sense. They moved within one week, possibly to another unit in the building, leaving a disgraceful mess behind, full cat litter box and all.

We eventually sold it to a doctor who was buying the condominium for his daughter, who was very spoiled and became a huge headache. She complained about the littlest things in a very whiny manner before her father finally closed on it. I called her "The Princess" to my staff and "Your Majesty" to her face when she had meltdowns and screamed at me to fix items that hardly needed replacing. We sell everything, including this unit "as-is," and it amazes me how many people, including highly educated medical doctors have no conception of this term. Because we were selling at such a high price point, the father insisted on a small number of items needing repair. I was willing to do so, but quickly regretted it. It seemed nothing was performed to their satisfaction, which I got the impression is an impossible task. For this reason I have learned to sell everything as-is, take it or leave it.

Sometimes tax deeds can resolve family or neighbor disputes. There was one gentleman who called himself the Buddha, claiming to be tortured over the use of a sideway to his property. Technically, he was unable to get to his garage without encroaching on the neighbors property. The encroachment was slight, approximately five feet or less. For over ten years the Buddha was granted unrestricted access, until the neighbor died and left the lot to her only son. The new heir never paid a single tax installment, and the land went directly into the tax sale. The son seemed more inter-ested in harassing the Buddha (and other neighbors) over the unauthorized use of the lot than redeeming the tax sale. His offers to sell or rent were unreasonable and nonnegotiable. The discussions felt more like extortion. It was unclear if he tried to sell it to the public or if he simply enjoyed the harass-ment. What is clear is that I sold it—to the Buddha—once a tax deed was issued. The Buddha, being a man of peace, allows the other neighbors to use the lot whenever they please, for free. He is not only a man of peace, but also a man of cash, and solved his problem through the tax sale system.

THE BAD

E VEN THOUGH MY glass is half full and I'm a very positive person, I can't ignore the bad. In fact, the bad times of life seem to outweigh the good, by about ten to one. It seems to me one needs to embrace those precious good moments, because they are few and far between. In the world of distressed property, this is an absolute truth. Perhaps this is another aspect the late night infomercials fail to mention when speaking on the subject. They may highlight the one good tax buy or foreclosure that is profitable, but you will never see any instructional book (other than this) explain in honest detail the bad parts, as that would ruin their pitch. I did not write this book to sell anything; I actually don't mind if you buy real estate or not. I am more interested in simply relaying what I have experienced. Learning from your mistakes is important, but learning from the mistakes of others is vital. So learn what you can here, because this chapter is dedicated to the very worst part of my job.

These stories range from bad to worse, and this chapter begins with the first really bad eviction I encountered.

It was a home in Calumet Park, Illinois, that had become vacant. The mail had been returned to us during the notice service period (the last six months before the final redemption date) and the yard became a jungle; the city began maintaining it and billing the amount towards the property. We had purchased the tax lien three years earlier, but it became vacant and run down during that time period. Even in poor condition, it was a nice single-family brick home. There was nothing materially wrong with the home; it was only neglected because the owner had passed away. I was unaware of this development until the sheriff evicted and I walked into the home. What I saw was an untouched death scene. The homeowner had passed away either in his bed or the hospital, as there was a clear trail from his bedroom where the stretcher was carried out leaving wheel marks on the carpet. Some furniture was moved to the side, amongst the prescription pill bottles scattered around. Most haunting was seeing his bed, which remained untouched—it was as if the paramedics took the body, closed the door and never looked back. I was the next person to go inside of the home, besides the sheriff who took less than five minutes to complete the eviction. Even though I had never met the man, he appeared to be a very nice person who was suffering from an awful disease. He had no family photos, and I surmised no family of his own; he seemed to be a hard-working man who went through life solo. On the kitchen counter were some get well cards, and I couldn't get over the calendar which he had marked on, up to his date of death. He was old school, the type that hangs the monthly calendar on the fridge and writes in dates of importance and reminders. Mostly there were doctor appointments and the crossing out of every day completed. It was almost as if he did that for a reason, to acknowledge another day of survival, another day of victory.

I dared not look in the fridge itself, though. I had learned this the hard way, should you ever purchase a vacant home with an old fridge, simply duct tape the doors and let the professionals burn it at once—do *not* open it under any circumstances. I repeat, do not open the fridge. The one time I did so, I regret forever. Maggots and mold had been growing because the power had been turned off, the smell of rotten food made me run outside and get physically sick. In this case, I had learned my lesson and didn't need to be reminded again.

I did not need to know this man personally to feel empathy for him. While we all die, it is probably hardest to die alone, with no one to claim your belongings or care about your passing. I was young and never considered this might actually happen to me, and now realize it very well may. Once the home was cleaned out, it was promptly sold. Though I was honest about what I had seen, the new buyer was unaffected; he did not see the photos of the man throughout the years or the haunting pill bottles all over the home, nor did he see that calendar which had every day of the month marked off until the day he passed. When you are sick and dying, days are all you have; yet when young you only think in terms of years. I was sick for weeks. A man I had never met, who simply failed to pay three years of property taxes over a fifty-year residency, had his belongings tossed out and hauled away with no one to grieve for him. Perhaps I did grieve for him; in some small way I felt as if I knew him, but in death—not life.

Soon after I was out in the field inspecting my current portfolio, which consisted of driving to each location and knocking on the door, trying to get a handle on why they were delinquent in property tax for so long. I was trying to be both motivational and helpful to get the homeowner to redeem. I had developed a script of sorts, which was tiring but beneficial as I noticed redemptions did increase. I said things like, "Come on, you can't lose your home for only a few years taxes, can you?" Or, "Why don't you try to refinance or sell the home and get something instead of losing it and getting nothing?" One day I pulled up to a home on the Southwest Side, and upon knocking, a young child answered the door, who was barely tall enough to open it. I was taken aback, but asked if I could speak to someone else there. Heartbreakingly she told me there was no one else there. She was alone, answering the door for a total stranger.

Unfortunately I found an alive-one in Hometown, Illinois, a middle class suburb of Chicago about twenty miles southwest of the city. This was an investment property for this guy (I can't call him a gentleman) who was involved in some very strange antics. First off, he had obtained a private mortgage from one of his friends (I believe a relative) who was in charge of paying the real estate tax. The friend did not do so, and they had three years to work out (argue) the situation amongst themselves. However, after the initial tax year was sold, there are two other tax years that become available during the three-year waiting period. Both the friend and the owner deferred the tax situation to one another, until the full three years had passed. If real estate taxes are $5,000 per year and you do not pay them until the last day of redemption you owe $15,000 plus interest (if any) and penalties. That amount is more than most people have, however, that is only approximately $415 per month. When unpaid for over three years it becomes to high a hurdle for most, and neither of these two had anything close to it. He called asking me to help work something out, which I agreed to, but my monthly payments were still too high for him. He asked if I would discount the amount he owed, but I had already paid the tax money to the county on his behalf, so that was impossible. He hired an attorney, who filed objections to our tax deed proceedings, but the case was very weak and they lost. They still refused to settle.

We moved for possession but until not after the building was vandalized, ransacked, and rendered unfit to occupy. He pulled all of the electrical wires out of the wall, carved X marks into the wood floor, removed all of the bathroom fixtures and every window in the home. When the sheriff arrived, and we took possession we immediately filed a police report. Short of catching the guy on video, there was not much we could do, but an investigation did occur. We have been victims of vandalism before, but usually they just take the copper pipes, hot water heaters, or anything that can be immediately recycled for cash. (This has been an epidemic since the foreclosure crisis. The amount of theft in vacant homes is overwhelming, supported by recycling centers who never ask how they got the copper pipes in the first place—and both should be criminally liable). It was obvious who committed the crime, because who else would carve an "X" into a wood floor, and who would even think to remove the windows? This home was sold within one month, but sold for far less than it should have.

We took over a four unit building in the Humboldt Park neighborhood, which I can only describe as a frozen home. I knew there was trouble when I saw the entire sidewalk frozen, but I still had no idea what was waiting for me. The pipes had burst due to vandals, and the water had been flowing at full blast, probably for months. No one in that area thought to call to report the issue, most of the residents were either too busy selling drugs or using them. We are not entitled to possession until we receive the deed from the court, and the city seemed unaware the water was pouring out from many of pipes, even though they were clearly tracking the amounts—they tried to get us to pay an overwhelming $8,000 bill. We were not legally responsible for any water charges before we obtained the deed, and they knew this, but that never stops them from trying. Why didn't they shut it off when it reached the $500 level? One must wonder why it never caused any alarm when it went unpaid and reached $2,500 of water charges, or even the $5,000 level. Perhaps at the $7,500 level they should have sent someone to go check out the building, but that would involve common sense. I suppose the water charges stopped at $8,000 only because the winter prevented any more water from flowing out, hence our frozen home. Every level of this home had frozen water stacked vertically from top to bottom, simply frozen in motion. The entire floor was covered in a layer of thick ice; the kitchen counters were unrecognizable, as was most of the entire basement. You had to crawl on top of the ice to identify the bathroom. This home was demolished; it could not be saved, and so sits another worthless vacant lot.

Photos of the frozen home that the city of
Chicago eventually demolished.

Another eviction took place on North Clark Street in Chicago, in the trendy Lincoln Park neighborhood. The condominium unit was in a high-rise building, and we had a very hard time getting in touch with the occupant. Once the deed was issued we even contacted the building management, telling them an eviction was forthcoming unless the occupant contacted us. I lost patience and the sheriff conducted the eviction. There were two large glass doors leading into the condo entrance, and it is a miracle the sheriff did not smash them into a million pieces. That was precisely what they wanted to do, until the building manager disgruntledly opened it with seconds to spare. Once we got inside, the building manager got the key to the unit and opened the door. The former owner was a very successful professional who worked in the arts. Though she had very good fashion sense; she had zero common sense. Personally, if I received a "Demand For Possession" enclosed with a tax deed to my home, I would immediately call the number listed. This is one task I would not procrastinate, but this person was clueless. The sheriff began taking her possessions out onto busy Clark Street, piling it up outside of the high-rise. The building manager called her at work, and amazingly she was very arrogant; she refused to answer and her assistant claimed she was in a meeting. The manager was frantic, telling the assistant to interrupt at once, that she was being evicted from her unit and the sheriff was moving her possessions to the street. It turned out she was standing next to the phone.

I received very angry looks and more than a few confrontations from the neighbors. They thought I was the devil, a truly evil human being. I asked one of the sheriff deputies to stop, that this wasn't right and all of her belongings were going to be stolen: but a very aggressive deputy yelled, "Stay out of it! She should have paid her taxes!" I agreed and did not argue, that was the goal after all, to take possession of this unit. (As mentioned, they have stopped this practice, and now give the occupant a "reasonable" amount of time to remove their belongings, which was a change for the better even though the law does not define "reasonable.") She really should have called me to prevent this, but eventually she arrived in a taxicab to find most of her belongings on Clark Street. Onlookers gawked and stared while she screamed at me at the top of her lungs. I cringe as I write this, but what choice did I have? I offered the number of a storage company and suggested she call them, which she did. She also called her attorney who threatened me nine ways to Sunday. I had my office send a copy of the tax deed to the attorney who called after checking the facts of the case and was mostly apologetic. (It's amazing how attorneys can immediately change their tone.) That eviction started somewhere around 9 a.m. and ended sometime around 10 p.m., when the unit finally became vacant and in our possession.

Sometime after that I conducted an eviction on the Northwest Side of Chicago. The guy was at home—actually he was always home. Unfortunately he was a drug addict, who was in the late stages of this disease. He was a large Eastern European man, well over 6 feet tall, a towering build compared to mine. But he was not intimidating at all, because he was totally emotionless. Looking into his eyes was like seeing through him; I have never seen such a chilling vacant stare. He was very easy to work with and somewhat confused, having called some family who seemed to be expecting this day would come. He did not have many possessions in the home and the move was completed within only a few hours. We stood face to face before he left, him looking down on me with an expressionless face. We said nothing. I wondered what drug he was on: weed is not strong enough to have that effect, cocaine or crack would have made him go crazy, meth would make him skinny, and alcohol would have made him angry. Heroin seemed to be the only answer. Drug addiction is a sad path, and I feel for anyone suffering the darkness it brings.

There was an elderly woman in her upper 80s who hadn't paid much of any bill for quite some time. She was very frail and sweet, living in a modest home, and I instantly wanted to help her. She did not want help, but she did not want to move either, despite losing ownership of the home to us for unpaid taxes. I went by the home monthly to check on her, and she would invite me inside. I would ask her if she had any plans to relocate and perhaps move to a location where she could be cared for. She looked around, pointing to the old photos of her with her deceased husband, looking me in the eyes, she said, "But I've got no where to go." I noticed it was cold in the home and she was wrapped in a blanket, so I had the heat turned on in the company's name, directing the monthly bills to the office. For over a year I did nothing, except check on her and get to know her, not bringing up the fact I owned the home, not forcing the issue or adding any more stress to her life. We paid the taxes, the power bill, and sent a crew to landscape during the summer. I gave her numbers of agencies to call if she ever needed help. She was very determined to be independent. On a rainy October day, I went to check on her, but she was gone. The home was untouched but hot, the heat running on full blast. Her time had expired, but her memory lives on to highlight the importance of compassion.

There is an attorney in Chicago who could use a dose of compassion (and karma); I am on record in a deposition defending an elderly woman whom he was trying to forcibly evict from her home. However, this woman *had* the money to pay in full what she owed. As I said on record, under oath, he and his client were more interested in kicking this elderly woman out of her home than accepting the money she owed. They already had plenty of money, it was simply pain and suffering they wanted to inflict for no reason at all. She did nothing personally to them; they did not even know her. He simply grinned with a crooked smile, taking delight in the adversity like a sadist. He was short and overweight, with thick glasses and a maniacal laugh. His awful personality complimented his physical appearance. He enjoyed the suffering of others.

Acting with compassion and having ethical and moral values is far more important than money. While you can't tell this to the attorney mentioned above, 999 out of every 1,000 people would agree with me on this point. The one evil villain of out 1,000 will fail to realize that we all die broke. "You can't take it with you," it has long been said. The money, or about half of it (after exemptions), will go directly to the government upon your death—and ironically to very same people who need assistance—the same ones they spend their lives taking it from. The earth spins in a circular rotation; what goes around comes around—it is not a coincidence; it is science.

I've delayed writing the last story of this chapter for several reasons, but it is a story that needs to be told. The outcome of which forever changed our approach to demands for possession. At the time our approach was an envelope with only two documents in it: a short letter demanding possession and a copy of the tax deed. When we ask the judge to issue an order for possession when an owner or occupant refuses to move (or refuses to call us with moving arrangements), the judge will likely allow an automatic stay. This can range from several weeks to several months, depending on their discretion. Once that date has passed, we can tender the order to the sheriff and wait in line for the eviction to occur. In this particular case, it would not have mattered what contents were mailed, since he never opened it. When we did evict, his home was spotless, almost staged, perhaps in an obsessive compulsive way. On the kitchen table were letters from our office all neatly stacked but never opened. The letters, organized in chronological order, took over three years to compile, as it was everything from the very first notification of tax delinquency to the very last demand for possession. There are many notices in between; including a personal visit from the sheriff to be sure everyone in the home has been notified. Of course, he didn't open any of the notifications, but he didn't need to—he knew exactly what they read.

We all handle stressful situations differently and certainly one approach I have seen is to ignore the problem. While this usually makes it worse in the future, in the present tense it makes it better. I have had some awfully lean years, but never spent more than I could afford and have never once carried a credit card balance in my life. However, I have seen people who do spend into oblivion; the need to amass material items outweighs the money on hand or logic behind the urge. I have noticed that once they receive the monthly credit card bill, there appears to be no rush to open it—rather it tends to sit on the counter or buried somewhere for days if not weeks. The contents were frightening, but even more so, the nightmare becomes worse every single day as interest ticks in perfect synch with the clock.

This was the strategy of this man who lived in Worth, Illinois. He had a lovely home, and as it turned out a very nice brother who had moved out of state. This was the home he was raised in, this gentleman having lived in only this home his entire life. It had no mortgage, and he only owed three years of taxes on it. He could have sold it and taken the proceeds to move into an apartment; he could have possibly qualified for a home equity loan, perhaps a reverse mortgage through a private lender. He chose to do nothing, however, which made his personal situation worse. I had a feeling he was choosing to do nothing, as upon every inspection the home was occupied and well cared for. I wrote optional notices and letters in bright orange envelopes that read "NOTICE OF TAX DELINQUENCY" stamped on them to resemble parking tickets. (I had gotten this idea from getting an actual parking ticket one time.)

And so, almost into the fourth year, the sheriff finally made his way to the home to conduct the eviction. While the man was expecting the day to come, he was not expecting it on *that* day. My portfolio manager Dan conducted the eviction and gave the man my number. Dan was the good cop, being helpful and compassionate on the scene, and I was to be the bad cop, being a bit of an impatient prick on the other end of the phone. This haunts me. He only asked for more time; he never disputed we owned the home, and he was very understanding of the situation. He was caught by surprise he said, not expecting it and wishing the sheriff or I had advised of the eviction sooner. The sheriff had only called me the day before, and in the late afternoon at that, telling us the eviction was scheduled. Had we mailed something to him, he would not have opened it anyway, nor would there have been time to even send overnight mail. I asked several times why he did not call me in advance? We have a cash-for-keys program in which we agree on a reasonable move date and if the home is left fairly clean and the keys are provided to us the occupant or former owner can obtain cash. The cash amount will range depending on their situation, the amount of time needed, and other factors. I had wanted to offer this to him, but now it was too late. He asked if he could stay in the home for a few more days, but that was impossible since he would retain possession, and we both knew it would necessitate another sheriff eviction—possibly months in the future. I told him since he hadn't paid a mortgage (or any type of rent or taxes in years) that he must have some money saved, but he said he had been unemployed for those same years and had less than $100 to his name. He left peacefully and stayed with a generous neighbor on their couch for approximately two nights.

I was very accommodating in telling him he could take as much time as he needed to move his belongings out of the home, even up to one month if he chose. I offered a few phone numbers of homeless shelters and suggest he call the village of Worth to see if there were any programs or assistance he might qualify for. It was very quiet for a few nights, and I had listed the property for sale on the MLS with no interior showings until we had moved his belongings out and cleaned out the home. Within a few days we received a call from an interested investor; a family that buys homes in the area and flips them. They didn't care much about the interior condition since that was their specialty but mostly wanted to be sure they were not buying a frozen home, as described earlier, or a totally gutted disaster. This was reasonable, so

I sent Mike to meet them on a Friday afternoon to show them the home, do a quick walk through (not disturbing his belongings), and hopefully secure a sale. I half expected the occupant to move back into the home anyway, in the same manner the gentleman on Superior Street had done to us years before. The home, however, was untouched. When Mike got to the garage, he saw a body lying in the car, lifeless. The keys were on the dashboard; the car had *not* been running to induce carbon monoxide poisoning. But there was a note, which Mike did not read—leaving immediately to call 911. When both the police and ambulance came, they declared the area a crime scene. Mike called to tell me the news, and we were both very upset to say the least. He mentioned to me that in over ten years working together this was the first time something like this occurred, he being more aware of the statistics than I. But neither of us thought it would have happened in this nice suburban area. A few hours later, I received a call from the police department, a detective wanted to speak with me. He told me that I was mentioned in the note and explained what had occurred. He would not read the note to me at that time, until the investigation was complete—for days I wondered what was said about me. We were all sleepless. Soon after I received a call from the man's brother who was out of state and had heard the news. I was apologetic, and he was both understanding and reassuring. The note as it turned out mentioned me in a positive way, simply requesting that time be given to allow his brother the opportunity to gather whatever belongings he wanted. His last wish was indeed carried out and approximately one month later his brother and family took the possessions, thanked us with hugs—and the home sold soon after.

This drastically changed the method in which we conduct evictions. For instance we now supply a full list of governmental programs and agencies that can offer services to those facing homelessness. This list not only includes names but phone numbers and addresses of each agency. There is help out there for those that need it. Many of the people I have encountered simply refuse help—and while we cannot force anyone to obtain it, my hope is to avoid a situation like this from ever happening again. Playing a role in someone's death, even a passive one, is a very heavy experience, full of regret, and it is something I hope to never experience again. If you want to get into this business, you'll need to be sure you can handle emotional situations like this.

The scene before the sheriff conducted this ill-fated eviction.

THE UNBELIEVABLE

THERE ARE TIMES even I can't believe what I am seeing. My head does a double take in an effort to contain the brain matter and the possibility my eyes may deceive me. But in fact, it is true, and I've learned to expect the unexpected. While doing an inspection at a property I saw a stolen ambulance, which was modified to sell drugs. Yes, a drug-dealing ambulance. People on the block would run to the emergency vehicle (possibly having a withdrawal emergency of their own) to buy drugs in much the same way that an ice cream truck attracts children to run into the street. The ambulance was not there longer than a minute or two before it fled off to the next block, its customers scattering in every direction. I had not seen such an efficient or brash way of selling drugs before. Most of the time there is a young man at the top of the block asking if you want anything. Should you say yes, he will communicate to another in the middle of the block, and upon your arrival the dealer will greet you for a five to ten second transaction. Most of the time the ambulance does not even pull to the side of the road, and I have been in the car waiting for a drug deal to finish, totally blocking the street, no one seeming to care their business is illegal. The city of Chicago, in a welcome effort to curtail drug sales on the street, installed cameras on the corners of the most active blocks. I believe this necessitated drug sales moving to the center of the block, away from the cameras. Years ago, the local residents assumed I must be in the neighborhood to buy something, but since the foreclosure crisis began, I believe they see me as a banker, so I do not get bothered nearly as much or as aggressively.

I conducted an inspection of a home on West Madison Avenue, which by sheer misfortune had a very eager prostitute standing out front. She was instantly smitten with me—or the thought of me as an interested buyer of her product. She tried to open the passenger door upon my arrival, which thankfully was locked. Then she began knocking on the window, pressing her breasts up against the glass. If you have ever taken liquid medication when sick or done a shot of alcohol you hate, your face may have had the very same expression mine did. I waved her off, saying no, but she was not interested in rejection (apparently prostitutes have not heard of the no-means-no rule). She started bidding against herself, first offering $20 for her services, then $15, and eventually $10. While I was uninterested I admired her business sense, and she would have been an excellent auctioneer had she chose a different career path.

Once I drove past a very attractive woman in a mini-skirt who appeared to be hitchhiking. She had an enormous lollipop, something out of a carnival, and was flagging cars down, saying "HEEEEEYYY" to anyone who was driving past. I knew immediately this woman was no prostitute, but unfortunately I had to inspect a tax lien on a building a few doors down. I turned the corner and stopped in front of the property only to find a number of police and unmarked squad cars waiting in both the street and alley. This was clearly a sting operation, the police having designated the most attractive female police officer to play the part of the prostitute. I sat and watched, unable to believe what I was seeing, it was *so* totally over the top. The police did not seem to care I was there. Compared to the actual prostitute I had encountered before, this woman was a perfect ten; and if the lollipop didn't give it away, her well kept appearance should have. Still, car after car slammed on their brakes and upon her direction turned into the street. Immediately they were busted—but in a very organized way, the police directing cars into the alley first to allow new cars to not be tipped off. It was a very efficient operation; the reactions of the customers were a mix of both shock and disappointment. While it was a very successful sting, I couldn't help feeling some of these men were entrapped in some way, their wildest dream turned into a nightmare.

On the topic of crime and punishment, we received a tax deed to a vacant lot at Twenty-Sixth and Sacramento, which is directly across from the Cook County Jail. I was nervous it would be a tough sell, if not impossible, as the view from the lot was of a barbed wire covered cement wall. I remembered wondering who in their right mind would purchase such a lot? A sale I thought, would be unbelievable. Standing there, I saw a few arms hanging out of the very small windows of their cell, dangling from high above. If one man's trash is another's treasure, then one man's vacant lot (when priced right) is the perfect home site for a corrections officer. The buyer, a veteran employee of the jail had turned a forty-five-minute commute into a walk across the street by building a small but affordable home on that land. Quite brilliant actually when you consider the stress and long hours those guards must endure.

I received a phone call one day from a gentleman wanting to redeem his taxes. Although the last day to redeem had technically passed, he was calling to see if I would accept a late payment and resolve the matter. I agreed, but asked how quickly I could get paid the money he owed. He didn't have it, he said, or he would have redeemed on time. However, he was waiting on a large check from a Hollywood production studio. "Yeah, yeah, yeah," I said. I recounted the horrors of my days in the film industry and how twenty-five years later I am still waiting on a check myself. He explained, "No, this is different. I'm an accomplished actor. You can look me up on IMDB." I said, "You're telling the wrong person," and simply asked him to call me if and when he received the money. Thinking that speaking to someone else might change his luck, he called right back. And change his luck it did, as he spoke to my brother who, as it turns out, was a big fan. This wasn't just an ordinary home; this was the childhood home of a prominent actor, who rose to fame in several hit movies in the 1980s. He wanted to save his family home for no other reason than sentimental value, he said. He tried to sell it once, many years before, but his asking price was too high. I noticed the MLS listing made mention of his celebrity status as a selling point for the home. Although I rarely watch film anymore, I basically grew up on the movies he was in. But, once I grew up, I can't recall seeing him on screen again. For the record, while the acting work he did was excellent, I believe he is still waiting on that check.

A tax lien can happen to anyone, not just celebrities, but politicians as well. We purchased the tax lien on a mayor's home. That is not a misprint. An elected mayor of a city did not pay his property taxes. I had no idea it was the mayors personal home when I placed my bid at the tax sale. It was very hard to get in contact with him; his blinds were always drawn and he ignored letters and sheriff visits. When I found out later, I was shocked at the irony. Most unbelievably, he did not redeem the tax sale. He called after the redemption period, agreeing this could be a newsworthy event and desperately seeking a resolution. We were not looking to evict the mayor, so a resolution sounded fine to me. A payment plan was reached, but it brought to light an important issue. If the mayor of a city doesn't pay his real estate taxes, his constituents may follow suit. The very same programs and services he oversees are funded in part by his tax dollars. Yes, property taxes are unreasonable, but he is the person responsible for them. There is so much waste in government, and when public officials are unable to pay their self-imposed, ridiculously high tax rates, what hope do the rest of us have?

We obtained a tax deed to a home on West Grace Street on the Northwest Side. The home itself was very nice, a long time family home that was lost to property taxes. There was only one grandson residing in there, and he was not willing to move out peacefully, pay the tax owed, or accept cash for keys. Unfortunately, I see this scenario far too often: A home with a paid off mortgage owned for years by hardworking grandparents left to children and possibly grandchildren. If the home is left to six people, five have usually moved on with their lives, some moving to other states, others starting families of their own. But there is always one child or grandchild who wants the free ride, refusing to work; and if they are employed spend their money on anything but the home. They often do not sell because the home was split six ways, which is usually not enough for everyone to agree. The other siblings or heirs do not want to pay taxes on a home they do not live in, and usually they will leave the utilities and taxes to the person who is living there. Of course, living for free is the best arrangement, and I have seen many homes that have been in a family for more than fifty years lost for a few years of unpaid tax. I try to explain that no matter where they move after we evict, they will have to pay rent somewhere. "The days of living for free are coming to an end," I often say. I try to use this as motivation, to get people to realize what they have and what they are losing. After three years of unpaid tax, the total on this home was around $15,000 and the occupant/heir barely had $500. The other five owners did not want to split that bill nor should they, and a tax deed was issued. However, this is not the unbelievable part; this was a very common scenario. Upon conducting the eviction we found explosives—including military rockets, live and dangerous—all over the home. We were unsure if the occupant was trying to explode the home or if they were leftover from his grandparents, perhaps items from the war. We had to call the Alcohol Tobacco and Firearms (ATF) department who essentially sent out a bomb squad. I give the agency credit for taking it very seriously and showing up fast. They disarmed and removed the explosives. It served as a reminder of the dangers that are faced in forceful evictions. The photos shown next are two examples of the explosives found in the home.

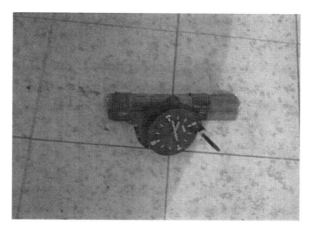

We encountered another dangerous and somewhat hilarious condition when we entered a home that had no electricity but was still being occupied. We found a number of tiki torches, the kind you might see in Hawaii or on a far away tropical island. But this was no tropical island; it was Stoney Island (Avenue), a main boulevard on the South East Side of Chicago. I give the occupants credit for using their imagination, but they neglected to realize tiki torches emit carbon monoxide and should only be used outside. A substitute for electricity these were not, and sadly no carbon monoxide or smoke detectors were found inside the home.

Another woman was an animal hoarder with a vast collection of both snakes and birds. Cages of animals filled the home, which angered me as an animal lover and activist. I read her the riot act and called a rescue organization for the animals, but in her sick and depraved mind she was caring for and loving these animals. I am no fan of snakes and felt very uneasy walking through this home once she was gone. These birds were not rare parrots; they were mostly pigeons kept inside and other local birds she had trapped. I have no idea where the snakes came from, as they are rare and not indigenous to Illinois, other than the harmless garden variety. This is a great example when a tax deed can be a beneficial as it can identify and eradicate abusive and neglectful behavior. The photo below shows the main room to give you an idea.

We have encountered many homes with squatters, some in high-end properties as previously mentioned, but most live on the very lowest end. Some have fake leases and sales agreements, claiming they are legally entitled to reside in the home, while others leave peacefully once they are caught. But I had never encountered squatters who only resided in the garage. The home was vacant, so they could have resided in the main home; but they lived neatly in the garage and felt entitled to do so. I explained, as did the sheriff, that the garage *is* actually part of the home, and they needed to move out. They acted a bit shocked, arguing with Mike and me about their right to possess the garage—even though it had an inoperable garage door and cement floor. You can see from the photo shown below they were very clean and respectful, clearly facing homelessness if not for the shelter of a frame garage with no heat or running water. This was a reminder of the harsh realities real people face on a daily basis.

Taking up residence in the garage.

We took over a home in a south suburb of Chicago, and in an effort to obtain a transfer stamp from the village (a requirement to record the deed upon a sale) were given a bill for $500 for a raccoon eviction. It only costs $250 for the sheriff to evict an actual human being, but twice that for a raccoon. This occurred before we owned the home, and we fought aggressively to remove the charge. They had hired a specialist who does not hurt the animal and simply relocates it, but the village had to pay him. They also sought over $1,500 in other maintenance fees, which they could not itemize, simply calling it an "Unpaid Invoice." In an effort to sell and make peace, we agreed to pay for the raccoon eviction, if the village removed the other fees, which they did. We were able to sell the home to the buyer, raccoon free. Below is the invoice we received, the address of the property redacted for privacy reasons.

DATE: August 1, 2013
DATE OF SERVICE: August 1, 2013

PROPERTY MAINTENANCE

Racoon Eviction	$ 500.00
Unpaid Invoice dated 06/25/13	1,048.60

There is an old mansion in the Hyde Park neighborhood, not far from where Barak Obama lives, that can best be described as a haunted house. The home has a Victorian look; it's approximately four stories with minarets and a veranda wrapping around the front and sides. At one time it must have been an amazing home for the only the most affluent Chicagoan, but it had since become unoccupied for years and fell into disrepair. It reminded me of the Munster's home from the old TV show with rain and lighting hovering over the home when it is otherwise sunny everywhere else. I had held the lien on this home for the full three years, and on the final redemption date, I went to the property once more. I had assumed there would be no redemption from the tax sale, since it was unoccupied. I had obviously invested substantial money into it—as well as time—but I was nervous since the taxes were so high on an unoccupied haunted-looking home. I met the neighbor who gave me the backstory and basically scared me to death. He had been inside, often just to keep it secure, telling me it needed a full rehab, as the roof had caved in and the home was full of junk. He was friendly with the family that had owned it and had permission to keep it secure and watch it for them. The owner had died and left it to three heirs—sisters, who hated each other. He showed me parts of the home; it was awful and smelled like mold; my allergies acted up for weeks. Other than a few others, this lien was one of the largest investments per dollar I had ever purchased. I was a bit over my head, not even sure if I could sell it for anything close to what my basis was. I drove home nervous and didn't sleep much, sneezing often and unable to get that mold and mildew smell out of my nose. The next morning, my assistant checked the redemption books at the county and found that a redemption on the tax lien was made! This included all of the tax we had paid plus approximately 12 percent interest per year for three years. The redemption literally came during the final hour, after 4:00 p.m. I was so grateful and relieved to have actually profited from this home and to have avoided the mess that was waiting for me. As it turned out, a competitor had acquired the rights of ownership from one of the sisters and redeemed the taxes on it—more that $80,000, not realizing he did not own the other two-thirds, nor was he ever going to. This investor highlights the reason people should not take risks in this arena; the pitfalls can be expensive if not disastrous. He had an attorney frantically call the office on his behalf almost begging us to not collect the redemption proceeds. Perhaps he paid a visit to the home himself, or perhaps he finally contacted the two other sisters, who, like me, were not taking his calls.

Speaking of haunted houses, I am often asked about the creepiest home I've ever seen—because I've seen some unbelievably creepy scenes. Once I bought the tax lien on a funeral parlor combined with an apartment building. The mortuary was operated from the first floor with apartments above and behind the building similar to an old style motel. The property was fairly well kept with an expansive parking area, which also meant a high tax bill. An ironic sign read, *Keep quiet at night.* I wondered who would live in such a place? I've lived in some crummy places and with some crummy neighbors—but thankfully they were at least alive. The apartments were mostly occupied, including by the owner who opted to use a modified coffin instead of a more traditional bed. I presumed he was being courteous, should his time expire, but it turned out the coffin was good for his back. He had a sense of humor, when asked why he couldn't pay his taxes he appeared dramatic and said, "Because business is always dead."

But the winner of the creepy award goes to someone I'll never know. His physical body may have been long gone by the time the sheriff arrived but his presence remained. This was a bone chilling, hair-raising, night-terror type of creepy. Imagine a mix between a twisted carnival show and haunted house. But with an adult twist. And though the sex, drugs, and wild rides were all but over, the evidence remained. This was clearly not your average party. It appeared professional. The first floor was used as a meeting room or socializing area, with a bar-style set up. The patrons were clearly in the mood for hard liquor, as empty bottles of alcohol were neatly lined up on the counter. A pile of used carnival tickets sat on a table, confirming paid admission. The apartments above hosted the action. One unit was particularly disturbing; only a mattress remained on the floor, with folding chairs surrounding it in a circle. A blanket lay amid a stained mattress cover, while various wigs were found in the closet. The mattress served as the stage, in a perverse theatre in the round. While likely not a Shakespearian performance, I am sure there were similar elements of both comedy and tragedy on display. After the performance, the patrons politely left, never to return. The scene, shown below, remained untouched until the sheriff conducted the eviction.

THE BAT-SHIT CRAZY

AH, THE MAIN event. There have been times in this business when I thought I'd seen it all—but then stories like these arise. These can't be categorized as unbelievable, because they are realistic and believable. There are many types of "crazy," and I am not trained to diagnose or treat the various mental health issues that these people face (if any). I have reported a few people to the authorities when I have been worried for either my safety or theirs, but I am unsure if any action was ever taken. I have seen people go "crazy" when very upset, but I consider that only temporary; when they calm down they return to normal. Perhaps that makes them bi-polar; perhaps they are just normal. I myself have a short fuse at times; the old saying "don't mess with a happy redhead" is very true. But crazy I am not. Maybe on some level we are all a little nuts, but for the purposes of this chapter, there is a specific headspace some people retreat to. It is located far-far away from the land of normal, and well beyond the land of the insane—a place that can only be described as bat-shit crazy.

Let's start with the paranoid—those that won't answer the phone, as they fear there may be someone else on the other end. These are the same ones who only find comfort within the four walls of their home and only venture out when absolutely necessary. During a routine inspection of a condominium unit we had a tax lien on, I encountered a very strange sign. It was posted on the door in large print. The sign, shown below, instructs everyone, including utility companies (who are only trying to supply them with power) to go away. However, the sign does not relieve them from paying their taxes, which had been unpaid for over two years. We must attempt to notify the owners and occupants since they can lose their property if they fail to redeem. Not only did I knock on that door, but also wrote my name and number at the bottom, as directed, but did not receive a call back. My visit worked, though, as they did redeem their property taxes within a few weeks.

Yes, I knocked—loudly.

A very sad situation happened in Bellwood, Illinois, which was highly publicized in the local news due to the nature of the violent crime: a murder. The man involved was sentenced to twenty years in prison for first-degree murder. The argument stemmed from something as simple as his wife inviting a friend over to the home who the husband suspected to be a thief. After the arrest, the son continued living in the home until the day of eviction, refusing to move and treating us with extreme disrespect. In his defense, this was a trauma I cannot imagine; but even so, I would not want to continue living in the same home where my father stabbed my mother to death. If you plan on buying foreclosures or tax liens, you need to be willing to inherit these gut wrenching realities and have a plan of action in advance to protect yourself and your investment.

Man convicted of fatally stabbing wife

A Bellwood man was found guilty Wednesday of first-degree murder for stabbing his wife to death during an alcohol-fueled argument in their home more than two years ago.

..............., 67, and his wife, ..., 52, were arguing Aug. 19, 2006, when they ran out of the house in the 500 block of 23rd Avenue and chased each other around the yard.

At least one witness who testified during the three-day bench trial in the Maybrook courthouse in Maywood said both were carrying knives when .... ran back into the house and locked the doors.

After a few minutes, he re-entered the house still carrying the knife. He confronted his wife in the dining room and stabbed her once through the heart.

The undisputed queen of the bat-shit crazy society goes to the woman in this next story. She was once a teacher for a Chicago Public School, but was terminated for giving a math exam to young children that was meant for an advanced graduate class in mathematics. Not one child in the class got even a single question correct, and when one broken hearted and traumatized student came home to show her father the exam, he went a little bat-shit crazy himself. He demanded an explanation from the principal. Now I am quite sure that principal had seen a lot of things, but never something so bizarre as a test given to fifth graders that rivaled an Ivy League examination in Advanced Algebra. This led to the teacher's dismissal, and although unemployment was offered to her, she refused to accept it. She believed the "system" was corrupt, so she refused to support the government in any form—which included paying property taxes on her investment property (which she had rented out).

Not knowing this backstory—or what I was about to get involved in—I was the winning bidder at the tax sale for a home located in a very good neighborhood at the 2600 Block of North Drake Street. When no redemption was made from the tax sale, we made application to the court to issue a tax deed, which she fought, representing herself in the proceedings. The judge, a very nice, compassionate, and patient man, asked her at one point if she had the money to pay the taxes. She replied that, yes, in fact she did—but that was not the point. She was upset at the corrupt system in which we live, and unfortunately she quickly identified me as a conspirator with the system, and my brother as my co-conspirator. Her filings were addressed to public officials: federal judges, the chairman of the FBI, the CIA, the President of the United States, and us.

On the day of the eviction, approximately six tenants fled quite willingly—she had rented the house by the room. She was arrested for assaulting a police officer and was led off to

Cook County Jail. She bailed herself out and immediately returned to the home to confront me. Her daughter was in the home at the time, working cordially with me to organize the belongings and move out the possessions. The woman called the police, saying I was stealing her home, repeating my name over and over and calling me a thief. The police showed up but quickly left, knowing I was not stealing anything. She called them again five minutes later. The captain of the force showed up personally and yelled at her, telling her he would take her to jail again if she didn't leave, and shaking his fist at her in anger. To my shock, she did leave, and I secured the building with a metal hasp and combination lock, thinking perhaps the situation was under control. I could not have been more wrong. She not only moved back in, but also wrote disturbing messages on the walls—how the sale of the home was a fraud and that it was under FBI investigation. Much more disturbingly, she set up booby traps that could have killed us—she was using war mentality. She reversed the flow of air on the forced air system so it would emit dangerous carbon monoxide inside of the home. Worse yet, she essentially did the same with the hot water heater, turning the appliance into a dangerous missile, ready to explode upon simply turning it on. Big Mike was experienced enough to alert me to this, or I would not be alive to write this story. Mike brought his very lovely and sweet mother along to keep watch while he essentially diffused the bomb. The woman locked both Mike and his mother inside the home, using her own pad locks to lock the doors from the outside where we had put the metal hasps. She crawled onto the roof and screamed violently in another language. Mike is very tough and was able to break the back door open from sheer force. He promptly called me. I called the police again, and she went back to jail. The detective told me she was a real piece of work once detained—I told him, "You have <u>no</u> idea." He read me her prior arrest record and it was shocking. She had left her child in a hot car one day, prompting police to break the window.

Because the home had value, we called a company specializing in vacant property security. They installed metal doors and screens on all windows and doors, making it impossible to penetrate without a color-coded combination. I was present with my German shepherd, Roxy, when they installed the doors and screens, a process that took over 4 hours. I had brought coffee and a newspaper and was very content waiting, knowing she would show up to cause trouble. They showed up and all was quiet for the first few hours. When the installers were inside working on the metal screens, she appeared, grabbed a box of much needed screws and bolts, and ran down the street with them. She returned a few minutes later, as if nothing happened, calling the police and claiming I had attacked her as well as stealing her home. You could tell the 911 operator was struggling to understand her: the only clear words were "Tim Gray is stealing." At first the 911 operator was on her side as she sounded like a victim of an emergency, for a moment I myself thought Tim Gray was an asshole. Soon you could tell the operator was giving up, as she kept yelling about the conspiracy and asking for help. She demanded the 911 operator not send the police, as they were also involved in the conspiracy, but only the FBI. She described me accurately, standing on the front porch but referred to Roxy as a husky. Being physically attacked and rigging a gas appliance to kill me is one thing, but calling Roxy a husky was simply over the line and uncalled for. While the screens and doors kept her out, she wrote the same disturbing messages on the outside of the building to alert the neighborhood that I was a fraud and was stealing her home.

This situation is an example where trying to be compassionate simply will not work. The issues she had and her struggles with mental health had nothing to do with me. She was very intelligent, just bat-shit-crazy. Next are a few photos from the awful scene.

*Photos of her defacing the property and
warning buyers of the alleged fraud.*

Roxy asking, "Who are you calling a Husky?"

Once the home was secured, it was an even harder task to sell it. Not only had it been defaced, but any potential buyer was scared to even walk inside. Most of the time she was there during the showings, telling prospective buyers the home was under FBI investigation. The home even caught the attention of a local social media enthusiast, who posted her own creative opinion of the home on Twitter, which was not far from reality.

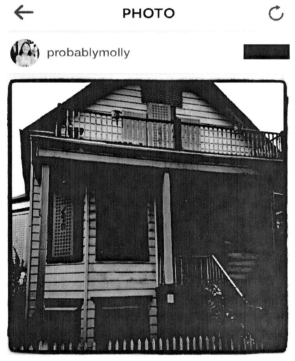

← **PHOTO** ↻

probablymolly

adamwishneusky, cwylie0

probablymolly This house is prepared for the zombie apocalypse, or it's the start of it.

Photo courtesy of Molly Marshall.

We eventually sold the home to an investor who was tough enough to handle it. It is worth noting that while I have felt corruption myself, and in some ways agree with her, her actions and methods are beyond reasonable. They were dangerous, life threatening, and illegal. While I appreciate her attempting to stand up for what she believes in, there are far better ways to start a revolution.

INTERMISSION

THIS SEEMS LIKE a good time to take an intermission, and share my photo collection with you. I have taken copious notes and photos of every tax lien we have ever purchased—literally tens of thousands of properties. These are the very best—or more accurately, the very worst from my experience in real estate. In going through and selecting only a portion of them, I had to make some tough calls. I wanted to show the reality of this business, untouched and raw. I refused to exploit the people themselves, and I had many more graphic and disturbing images of the people involved—including crime scene photos. Since this book is really about the homes themselves, including those did not seem appropriate. There has been no editing or staging of any of these photos and the properties were exactly as we found them. In most cases we have corrected the dangerous conditions, but in some, we simply sold the property in its "as-is" condition.

Selecting these photos brought back memories I had simply blocked out, like one of the hoarders, who had called after the eviction asking if he could get some things out of the home. I told him he was welcome to get whatever he wanted if he could find it in the mountain of trash; and commented that his home was the among the worst I had even seen. I asked how he could have endured living in such awful conditions. He paused to reflect and told me that he hadn't intended for the home to get so bad, but that it slowly got out of control. In the foreclosure world, we mostly witness the very end of such a personal struggle, whether drugs, depression, or hoarding. The most fascinating aspect is that for every end there literally is a new beginning—a new owner ready to start from the ground up and begin anew. It is also a chance for the former owner to begin again, to recognize the actions that led to this demise, and take action to live a better life in the future.

One day this home was a quality tax lien; the
next day it was a charred disaster.

The Chicago style after school special

You paid for this

Looks like it may be time for this resident to move.

Someone stole the radiators from this home
(notice the lock still intact).

Plenty of sunlight and fresh air in this foreclosure. (We did not purchase this home at the tax sale, but one of my competitors did.)

This takes the drive-thru window concept to another level.

Housekeeping, the sheets need changing! (Notice the bags attempting to keep the clothes clean in the background.)

Just when you thought it couldn't get worse: this bedroom was occupied at the time of eviction.

A sobering moment from a loving daughter.

A heartbreaking memorial for a child on the West Side of Chicago.

*An occupied master bedroom; the occupant
actually wanted to stay here.*

Needles are one of the most dangerous
hazards in the foreclosure industry

This is why we can't have nice things.

Allow me to freshen up!

*The water bottles were used to flush the
toilet after the water was shut off.*

After that last photo, we need a laugh, and some soap.

THIS BAR GOT
RAIDED BY THE
COPS WHILE I
WAS HERE!
WTF

Bad timing for the inspector.

From the outside this looks like a very nice two flat with curb appeal; so we obtained the tax deed...

But this is the inside of the very same home after the eviction.

And then the city demolished the building a few months later, as shown below.

Another home that looked great on the outside.

And another

Yes, that is a FOR SALE sign on the door.

*This home was sold at the tax sale to a competitor highlighting
the importance of quality tax sale preparation.*

No permit found for this botched porch job.

A few examples of hoarding. I have enough
material for an entire book on the subject.

That's not a closet!

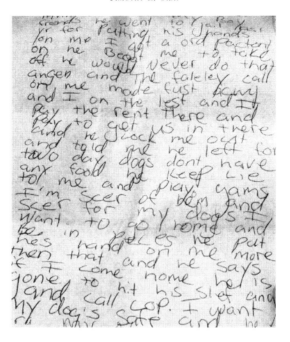

An official statement from an occupant filing a police report.

A payphone in a house is somewhat brilliant.

*Still want to get into this business? This is what
it takes to prepare for just one tax sale.*

An example of a tax lien certificate of purchase, this is what you receive as a winning bidder at the tax sale. The original must be turned in to either collect the redemption money or to obtain a tax deed from the court.

E ½ SE ¼ SEC 18-38-14
LAKE

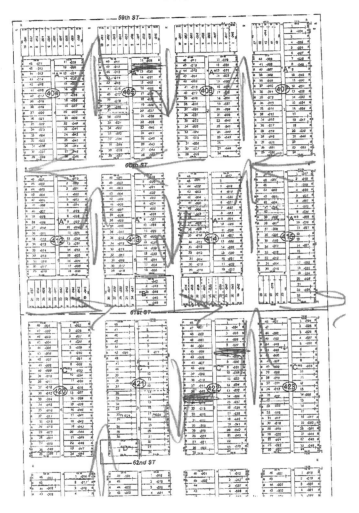

An example of a Sidwell tax map used to do property inspections before the tax sale. The arrows notate one-way streets and the subject property is highlighted. We inspect hundreds of properties per day, per inspector.

On Assignment with Roxy.

This is how I celebrate the end of a great tax sale.

THE TRICKSTERS

SOPHOCLES WROTE: IT is better to fail with honor than succeed by fraud. Centuries later, this statement has not lost its meaning; it quite possibly means more now than ever. Integrity and ethics are important themes of this book, as they are the guiding principles of my life. In the electronic era in which we live, it is much easier than ever to identify and prosecute fraud. However, due to online groups that serve as meeting places for like-minded criminals, hackers, and extremist, there is an alarming amount of growth in this arena. Many citizens who are frustrated and angry seek the safety and security of others who only fuel their feelings with conspiracy theories and fraudulent schemes. Years ago a friend of mine did three nights in jail for a repeated traffic offense; he came out an expert on car theft, drug smuggling and lock picking. While there is no honor among thieves, there certainly is a willingness to share information. If relayed to a desperate, feeble-minded individual, the information can become very dangerous. "He knows every trick in the book," assumes there is an actual book of tricks and scams to learn and apply to perpetrate fraud. The "book" is essentially available on the Internet; and with the invention of scanners, color printers, and electronic deposits, this very "book of tricks" has become a form of domestic terrorism. At the risk of enlightening future criminals to the schemes in this chapter, I have decided to publish my experiences: knowledge is power for both sides. All of these examples were regrettable by the offender, as they chose the wrong person to victimize. In some of these cases I wonder how anyone could imagine these schemes would be effective.

Most recently I've had to deal with three separate incidents (one year apart) that took place at the same building, located in a high crime area of Chicago. The streets are filled with many good citizens but also a substantial portion of rogue warriors who have their own version of law and order. The building was formerly owned by a well-known gang member who had been sent to prison. We were the unsuspecting new owners of the apartment building, a place targeted by other criminals and gang members, possibly for revenge. It started with the sale of drugs in the garage, which at one time was a coach house. Once we found out about the illegal activity, we called our friends to install their metal doors and screens. The usually impenetrable steel was compromised; the first of three offenders was caught in the act, attempting to remove the steel from a window and resell it. This, as I have found, is the biggest issue Chicago faces in vandalism: recycling centers that pay cash to anyone who has metal or copper to sell. The owners of these recycling centers never ask *how* or *where* they obtained the steel (these were clearly marked) or why someone has various copper pipes that were obviously stolen. They simply weigh the metal and pay cash on the spot. This needs to be eradicated immediately and outlawed within the city limits, so that these criminals have to travel to the suburbs or show a receipt for the metal before payment is made. The police had this building on their radar and drove by often, arresting the offender, who was a veteran of the armed forces. His defense was that I had given him permission to remove the steel, so the officer called me to confirm. At first I laughed, as did the detective. I stopped laughing when told he used my name—not my company name, but my personal name. Since he was a veteran, he was eligible for a program of rehabilitation, which he accepted. We had listed the building for sale, but due to the high crime area had a very hard time selling it (it took two years). A few months later, I got a call from the same detective; there was another arrest at the building—the offender was stealing the pipes from the basement. The police caught him leaving the property with handfuls of copper, their guns pointed directly at him. The first words out of his mouth were, "Timothy Gray told me I could take these pipes." The detective arrested him after confirmation from me no authorization was ever given. He asked if I was willing to testify against him, which I was, and subsequently the court issued a subpoena. I showed up on the day of trial to offer my testimony. The experience was hard to endure; the criminal courthouse is not for the weak of heart. I was there over eight hours, refusing to eat lunch, as my options were not appetizing (hot dogs floating in dirty water). No cell phones were allowed, so that meant I was bored out of my mind. I spent half the day with the detectives; trading stories and making them show me their guns. The other half of the day I sat in the courtroom and watched criminal after criminal appear in their beige jumpsuit, taking plea bargain agreements or listening to their attorneys asking for continuances. I probably saw more than one hundred total years in prison handed out in a few short hours. Weak with hunger and agitated, I testified and did a fine job. I left thinking I would never return. The man stared at me with ice-cold eyes while I told the court my side of the story. He was found guilty and given 6 years in prison. He was sent to Statesville Prison, a notoriously tough prison.

Less than two weeks later, the very same detective called, and once again, another arrest at the building. The detective had my number on speed dial at this point. This time it was a well-known career criminal, who claimed I had hired him to remove the pipes in the building. He again, used my full name. I have come to discover they simply used Google to search for the address and saw I was the listing agent. Perhaps realtors who sell bank owned properties simply do not care and would not be bothered to show up all day and testify at a trial. All three of these criminals chose the wrong person. On the third occasion, I waited at the court for hours only to find the case was continued. Months later, I was told to return. I was present, a witness was present, the detectives were present, and the case was ready for trial. Moments before the case was called, in an effort to frustrate and aggravate all of us, the public defender requested another continuance. It's an old parlor trick in the Circus Court: the public defender juggling on a tightrope and turning me into the rodeo clown. This case is still pending, but I will return as needed or, as I was told, a warrant will be issued for my arrest—what irony.

Now, let's shift gears to a slightly more sophisticated scheme. Take a look at this next check; it is fraudulent.

To the naked eye this looks like a legitimate check. The owner of the property was attempting to settle her tax lien in the amount of $23,500. The fraud department of our bank notified us about the check and called the fraud department at PNC who said, "This check is as fake as the day is long." To begin with, the numbers at the bottom are totally nonsensical. The check number in the top right is fictitious as is the number printed on the top left. An actual cashiers check from PNC Bank does not look anything like this, but other than working for the bank or being a customer you wouldn't have that information. I will be the first to admit it was shocking to me, especially since the bank assumed I was involved in the fraud since we deposited the check. Cashiers check fraud is the most common type of bank fraud used in electronic transactions, especially for eBay and other auction sites. The idea behind the scheme is a simple matter of timing: the goods have usually been shipped before the seller is alerted to the fraud. In this case, we were in the process of canceling the tax certificate when notified the check was fraudulent. I have to wonder why they did not go to jail for this; they did not even seem remorseful. Shockingly they did appear in court when we presented the evidence to the judge to reinstate the tax deed case. They claimed a family member got the check on their behalf, faulting the family completely. This is a great example of playing dumb, even when caught red handed.

The remaining stories in this chapter deal with people who somehow think they can outsmart the system. Some of these people do have intelligence, and it occurs to me that if they spent the same amount of time learning a trade and applied themselves, they may have the ability to pay their property taxes.

Next is an example of a disgruntled condominium owner who was considered a "rogue tenant." He intercepted the monthly assessment check we sent to the condo association, which is a federal crime in itself, but instead of cashing the check, he sent it back by Certified Mail. He was of the opinion that the condominium association was not complying with the law, even though it was. As such, he made up his own condominium association—using his imagination—and made himself the secretary. Since it was all in his mind, I wonder why he didn't make himself the president of the association, but perhaps he reserved that position for his imaginary friend. In his correspondence, he asked for copies of various personal documents, a red flag for fraud and possibly identity theft. At the end, he fails to even sign the letter, perhaps believing that would indemnify him from prosecution.

By far, the most troubling case of fraud occurred when a woman created a fraudulent deed with my signature on it. It was in the form of a quitclaim deed that purported to transfer a property from myself to her. She was not the former owner of the home, but she chose to involve herself in the property, committing what would have been a felony had the police taken the time to make an arrest. She had the deed notarized and recorded with the Cook County recorder. Although it should be pointed out that for a small fee the recorder will record a love letter and apply it to a property. Perhaps the police did not arrest her because the deed was such an obvious fraud, almost embarrassing for her. For starters, I did not own it; my company did. My name only owns one home: the one I live in. My company owns the rest of the property, but this never occurred to her. She would have known Wheeler owned it had she checked the title. It was bewildering, the handwriting used for my signature was the same as that for hers, not to mention the signature was not even close to mine. She attempted to convey a home I never owned back to her for no money, and somehow believed this would be legitimate.

Most alarming was the assistance of the notary, who was clearly involved in the scheme. I reported that person to the National Notary Association and am unaware if any action was taken. The entire point of a notary is to have an independent person who is professionally licensed with the state bear witness to both parties executing the document. For them to have recorded this blatant forgery on the title is an amazing act of stupidity and shameless greed.

Below is the actual quitclaim deed that she used and recorded showing that I personally transferred the property to her, even though I never actually owned it. A quitclaim deed simply transfers ones ownership to another; it does not warrant against any title deficiencies and is most common when transferring property among family members or when you want to be removed from any liability. She later admitted to me that she was "having problems" at that time in her life, but that was only after she had shown up later at an auction I was conducting and was the winning bidder on a property I was selling. She was obsessed with me and not in a good way. Just my luck: the one woman who is obsessed with me creates a forgery and becomes a nightmare. She tendered $5,000 on that property during an auction I was working, but until the auction was over I did not notice it was actually her. The auction was to a packed house and she sat in the back of the room. After I notified the authorities, she wisely gave up and went away for good. Although this example below seems comical, she was never prosecuted; the notary to my knowledge was not either, as I was never called to testify against either of them. It created problems for me, however, necessitating the filing of an affidavit and making the future buyer uneasy about purchasing the home. The title company requested an affidavit, and they would not issue a title commitment without it. The buyer was not comfortable buying a home with fraud recorded on the title, nor was the title company comfortable insuring it. You cannot erase a recorded document; you can only amend it or record an affidavit explaining the mistake. Both documents are available to the public forever, and shown below.

GEORGE E. COLE®   No. 822 REC
LEGAL FORMS   December 1999

QUIT CLAIM DEED
Statutory (Illinois)
(Individual to Individual)

CAUTION: Consult a lawyer before using or
acting under this form. Neither the
publisher nor the seller of this form makes
any warranty with respect thereto, including
any warranty of merchantability or fitness
for a particular purpose.

THE GRANTOR(S)   *TIM GRAY*

of the City *Chicago* County of *Cook* State of *Illinois* for the

consideration of *Ten + 00/100* DOLLARS, and other good and valuable

consideration, _____ in hand paid, CONVEY(S) _____ and QUIT CLAIM(S)

_____ TO _____ *Dr.*

(Name and Address of Grantees)

Above Space for Recorder's use only

all interest in the following described Real Estate, the real estate situated in _____ County, Illinois,

commonly known as _____ (or address) legally described as

See Attached

hereby releasing and waiving all rights under and by virtue of the Homestead Exemption Laws of the State of Illinois.

Permanent Real Estate Index Number(s) _____ - _____ - _____ - 0000

Address(es) of Real Estate _____ *Dr.*

DATED this *04th* day of *July*, 2004

TiMGRay (SEAL) _____ (SEAL)

Please
print or
type name(s)
below
signature(s)

_____ (SEAL) _____ (SEAL)

State of Illinois, County of *Cook* ss. I, the undersigned, a Notary Public in and for said County,

in the State aforesaid, DO HEREBY CERTIFY that *TIM Gray*

personally known to me to be the same person _____ whose name _____ subscribed to the

foregoing instrument, appeared before me this day in person, and acknowledged that _____ h _____

IMPRESS
SEAL

signed, sealed and delivered the said instrument as _____ free and voluntary act, for the

uses and purposes therein set forth, including the release and waiver of the right of homestead.

"OFFICIAL SEAL"
Notary Public, State of Illinois
My Commission Expires August 14, 2005

133

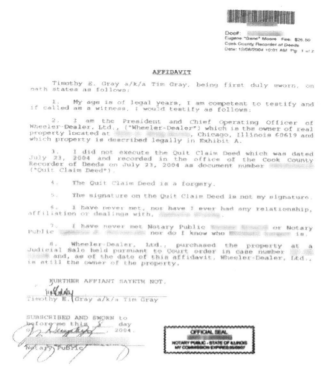

Finally, this chapter ends with the most bizarre scheme in modern history; it is run by a group of extremists known collectively as sovereign citizens. These are the class clowns of the fraud world, the ones who feel conspiracy theories are not potent enough for them—they live in a world of their own, as expatriates who forgot to leave the country. They feel that although they live in this county and use the public streets, emergency services, military (for their protection), and unemployment, they do not need to pay any type of tax. They claim they are a nation among themselves, exempt from the United States Constitution. Since I am in the property tax business, I have seen this theory tested from these clowns and have seen judge after judge give them the good ol' constitutional smack down. They are ever-present, however, their game seems to be ending; a federal judge in Chicago recently sentenced a sovereign citizen to many years in prison for recording falsified liens against another judge. The FBI refers to this scheme as form of domestic terrorism, which I agree with, but I also find some domestic comedy involved as well.

I have included three examples of this form of domestic comedy, all of which are similar but different. The first refers to a declaration of a "land patent" taking their theory way, way back into the time machine, before the United States Constitution was written. The second is more of the standard fare of the sovereign citizen, which is known as an "acceptance for value" scam. The final example is most puzzling, taking the approach that if you tender a fake check that is never cashed but not returned to you, the debt is simply discharged. They are all head scratchers, and we will highlight them one by one. Let's start with Mr. Land Patent, since his theory goes back the farthest in time.

DECLARATION OF LAND PATENT

ALLODIAL TITLE

I ▓▓▓▓ Deposes And say the following, through an extensive search of Organic Laws of the United States of America, including two hundred years of case laws of the (common laws), hereby claim the land on which my domicile now rests. "**Being a Real Person**" or Sovereign States Citizen I no longer Represent the "**Straw Man**" or (Legal Fiction) that is the individual described on my Birth Certificate, State I.D Voter Registration, and other so called Legal Documents. This independence has been inspired from the true Legal Stand point of the U.S Constitution, which **Gives** me Unalienable rights pertaining to the **Land** Thus Stated. I now describe Stated property from its original patent which was documented July 16, 1872 before the land was sold to J.D Parker who transformed this land into a sub-division that is legally described as the west nine (9) acres of that part. (The west nine (9) Acres of that part except the strip deeded to the Chicago Union Railroad Company, ▓▓ ▓▓ ▓▓ of the east half (1/2) of the west half (1/2) of the south east quarter (▓▓) in section (▓▓) Township (▓▓) north, range (▓▓) north, range (▓▓) east of the third Principal Meridian which lies north of west lake street). This is an official Revised and Amended version of the original land Patent or (Deed) of Stated Property. I ▓▓▓▓▓ now Explicitly express my Declaration of land Patent, which enforces and creates an Allodial Title in one name of a "Real Person" ▓▓▓▓▓

In this case, the gentleman is claiming he does not need to pay tax since he is using the "straw man" approach to his land patent. The straw man theory is a bit like having an alter ego: one persona is law abiding, but the other refuses to pay tax or be part of a society. The straw man is only a legal persona. Accordingly, the debt should only be paid by the straw man not the individual. Some take it as far as actually using two different variations of their own name; the imaginary persona is responsible for the debt the actual person is not. Taken from the Federal Bureau of Investigation website:

> Individuals promoting this scam frequently cite various discredited legal theories and may refer to the scheme as "Redemption," "Strawman," or "Acceptance for Value." Trainers and websites will often charge large fees for "kits" that teach individuals how to perpetrate this scheme. They will often imply that others have had great success in discharging debt and purchasing merchandise such as cars and homes. Failures to implement the scheme successfully are attributed to individuals not following instructions in a specific order or not filing paperwork at correct times.

Moving onward to the next sovereign citizen who did not want to pay his property tax, he attempted the use of the "acceptance for value" scam to avoid being held accountable for paying on his home. His method was in conveying the message, "Silence is estoppel by acquiescence." Yea, it makes no sense to me either. The argument is weak, but it states that if you are silent about his denial of debt you give consent to it. In similar fashion to the forthcoming third example, both feel that being nonresponsive will allow a discharge of all debt that is owed. In other words, as long as I write meaningless legalese to my mortgage company and they do not respond, my mortgage will be considered satisfied. Wouldn't that be so nice? Imagine the low wattage light bulb that goes off over their heads when they actually purchase and pay money for a program that teaches them this nonsense. I wonder why they don't write the teachers of this fraud the same letter and fail to pay for the instructional tapes, since "silence is estoppel by acquiescence" after all. To his credit, when he saw a number of his peers sentenced to prison for attempting such a scam, he abandoned the nonsensical theory before it got ugly— as well as the property, actually. In all cases, to avoid their humiliation I have redacted their names and addresses from their meaningless writing; although I certainly could include it, I do not feel it is necessary for this purpose.

June 19, 2014

c/o
Harvey, Illinois Republic c[60426]cf

NOTICE TO PRINCIPAL IS NOTICE TO ALL AGENTS IN THEIR PRIVATE CAPACITY
NOTICE TO AGENTS IS NOTICE TO ALL PRINCIPALS IN THEIR PRIVATE CAPACITY
SILENCE IS ESTOPPEL BY ACQUIESENCE

Certified Mail- 7014 0510 0002 2214 7648

RE: WHEELER FINANCIAL, INC.
Chicago, Illinois 60602

Dear Tim Gray/To Whom It May Concern:
Take notice and be advised that the alleged delinquent taxes for the year 2009 levied against the property addressed: HARVEY, IL. 60426 (Property Identification Number 0000) has been administratively discharged. Charges have been accepted for value and returned for full settlement/discharge and closure of demand presentment letter for Property Identification Number -0000.

I, , Third Party Interest Intervener and Executor of -
have not accepted any unlawful or fraudulent contract, or its conditions, related to the above mentioned property. I have accepted for value 2009 Tax invoice ORDER NO. and honor it with a negotiable discharge instrument as the *remedy provided by law*.

International Promissory Note Document No. is tendered in full amount for full settlement and adjustment of Property Identification Number . Complete execution of administrative remedy has been provided as proof. There is no further action needed to be taken on your part.

Note: You have 10 days to respond after receipt of this written correspondence, if so compelled. Non-response will be considered as compliance.

Sincerely Yours,

, Third Party Interest Intervener, Executor of

I enjoy this next example the most, if for no other reason than because the Secretary of State of Illinois basically shoved this right up the sovereign citizen's ass, warning he is going right to prison if he continues sending nonsensical letters to their department. I am not sure what the instructors of this ridiculous scheme would say about this letter from the Illinois Secretary of State, but generally when you get a cease and desist from a government agency with a warning you are going to do federal time, it is not good. I would think this would deter this sovereign citizen, but in fact it did not, it actually got him more excited to try to get out of the tax situation. This property is a large auto body shop with many apartments, and he owed almost $60,000 in taxes. This is not a single-family owner occupied situation. If he does not think he is responsible for property taxes running a large operation and collecting rent, I am not sure what in his mind would necessitate tax. And if no one paid their taxes, even if his view is right, what would the roads, schools, streetlights, and police presence look like? While it may save him $60,000 over the course of three years, the world would effectively come to a quick and horrible end for everyone. I am the first to agree taxes are too high; we get taxed on our income, on our property, on everything we purchase, extra tax on alcohol, smokes, even bottled water in Chicago—the more you make the more you get taxed; it is a wonder any of us have any money left over. But still if no one pays anything, we are truly in an awful situation. Yet, this sovereign citizen will not give up. He's convinced he has outsmarted the rest of us—that is until he finds himself having lost ownership of his property or even worse, his freedom.

OFFICE OF THE SECRETARY OF STATE

JESSE WHITE • Secretary of State

March 13, 2013

Chicago, IL 60617

Dear Sir/Madam:

Enclosed please find documents you recently submitted to the Office of the Illinois Secretary of State for filing under the Uniform Commercial Code (the "UCC"). Pursuant to Section 9-516 of the UCC, the Secretary of State is rejecting these documents. 810 ILCS 5/9-516. You will find your payment for the attempted filing and a list of the documents attached as Exhibit A.

Article Nine of the UCC governs secured transactions. A secured transaction takes place, for example, when one business extends credit to another in exchange for a security interest in some collateral. The secured party records the relationship with our agency to put other businesses on notice that it has a priority interest in said collateral. Banks, lending companies, and other businesses use this information when determining whether to extend the debtor future credit.

The documents you submitted do not appear to relate to a legitimate secured transaction. Please be advised that Section 9-501.1 of the UCC, effective July 20, 2012, provides for both criminal and civil sanctions for communicating false records to the filing office. You are hereby directed to **CEASE AND DESIST** from submitting non-conforming UCC documents with the Office of the Illinois Secretary of State. Continued attempts to file these documents will result in referral to the appropriate law enforcement personnel for prosecution.

Respectfully,

This statement, upon presentation to the filing officer, is considered to be FILED FOR RECORDS in accordance with Illinois Compiled Statutes, Commercial Code UCC ILCS & 0-401 and &9-403(1). See Study Comment (1)

The Office of the General Counsel

100 W. Randolph Street
James R. Thompson Center
Chicago, Illinois 60601
(312) 814-2762

THE RENTERS

T HE REMAINDER OF this book is slightly more informational. These renters have given me quite the education after all. The idea seems so easy; you buy a home, rent it out, collecting monthly income all the way to the American Dream. Easy that is, until they inform you they don't have the rent. At first they will say they get paid on the tenth, or later, and ask if you can wait for the money. Sometimes they will tell you they lost their job or had a family emergency with their kids or parents and simply cannot make ends meet. Well, perhaps you have a mortgage or some other bill to pay. What do you do? You could yell and threaten them but that won't help. You could be motivational, but generally there is a reason they are renting in the first place. If they are young then you should have some serious concerns about their maturity level. If they are older, then you really need to be concerned about why they are still renting at that age. Why don't they have anything in their savings account? Although you want to be compassionate, you also want to make ends meet. You will want to collect both first and last months rent right away. Security deposits are worthless, since you are restricted from using the security deposit as rent when they do not pay. Anyway, who can't fix some minor damage to carpet or drywall? The "move-in fee" is where it's at, and it gives you some extra insurance if they do not pay for a month. If the prospective tenant does not have two months of rent and a move in fee, do you really want to rent to them? I suggest screening the renter's credit, conducting a background check, and if possible, meeting them at their existing apartment. I have found this a great way to see how the tenant lives, because if they have cockroaches in their existing unit, they will be bringing them to their new apartment. Bedbugs also enjoy the excitement of travel. If they can't bother cleaning up their apartment and live in a sloppy fashion, you do not want to rent to them. The stakes are high, as I have found out, especially when the tenant is constantly getting high. In one instance I caught a tenant in the beginning stages of growing weed, which could create a legal problem for me, including the risk of losing the property entirely. Trying to grow weed is not only against the law in Illinois; it's also a reason to terminate the lease. This tenant claimed it was for medicine, that both he and his child had *a* sickle cell. "*A* sickle cell?" I repeated? "Yes, one of our cells is sickle." Having heard of the disease I tried to hide my laughter, because I know it is terrible for those affected. However, a basis for growing grass this was not. You cannot drug test an applicant but by going over to their apartment prior to approving them you may be able to get a sense if they smoke the day away. It is harder to identify cocaine and heroin addictions, which are far worse, but if the place is full of mirrors or if you see lots of people in the unit, it could be cause for alarm. Notice the music level and the type of stereo system while there. In one case I purposely left the application at the prospective tenants apartment, came back ten minutes later to find a two foot bong in full session, with "Insane in the Brain" by Cypress Hill blaring so loudly I could hear it from the street. You can always ask: Why are you moving?

Did I mention maintenance? You also need to be careful about the overall cost associated with the unit. One of the main pitfalls I see is with condominium assessments. These units will substantially cut into your profit, especially in a building with an elevator, as the repair and other common area expenses can run high. When you add in the mortgage, monthly assessment, real estate taxes, and insurance you are likely at the break-even level. My suggestion is to pay cash for your investment property and not to mortgage it, and if you are unable to do so, then do not involve yourself in the rental process. Many people disagree with this philosophy, but eventually the renter will move out or not pay, and you will lose a month or more of rent. You will need to be able to pay those bills even if the renter is giving you nothing. As mentioned earlier, I had one renter fail to pay for over a year, and while I obtained a judgment against him, collecting from someone who has nothing can be tricky.

I encourage anyone planning on renting out a property to come up with your own rules and regulations that will become an addendum to the lease. Loud music, harassment, lock outs, unauthorized occupants, smoking, and changes of cell phone numbers without notice to the landlord are all violations that can immediate terminate the lease. Strangely, these are embarrassingly absent in the standard leases you can buy over the counter, so an addendum is required. These rules range from mandating all animals have flea and tick medication (with documented proof) or that all animals must be walked outside of the home (in someone else's yard, not yours). I had to deal with this violation once. I took baggies to collect the dogs waste—and left it all for the tenant on their back door, along with a five-day notice.

I had one tenant, who used her deep fryer to cook chicken, but forgot she left it on and went to work. Within the hour the fire department called and the building was in flames. Thankfully the Chicago Fire Department did an incredible job, they were able to save the building with only the kitchen in one apartment damaged. After repairing the unit it dawned on me to disallow deep fryers in all of the apartment units we own. We added this to the rules and regulations and mailed notices. The tenant was irate, yelling at me over the phone, "You can't take away my chicken!" "I am not trying to take away your chicken, ma'am. I am taking away the deep fryer."

One of the major red flags with prospective tenants occurs when they need an apartment quickly. If you feel any pressure from them, if they seem frantic in anyway, then run like hell in the opposite direction. If they are not responsible enough to secure an apartment well in advance, they are most likely trouble. Worse, they could be running from creditors, being evicted, or possibly living in a hotel.

If you rent to Section 8 tenants (government subsidies) you may have to pay for their heat. I noticed the heating bill from a Section 8 tenant that was out of control considering the square footage of the unit. On a cold January afternoon, I paid them a surprise visit. I was shocked when a teenage child answered the door without his shirt on. The outside temperature was less than ten degrees, but inside it was set to a tropical 80 degrees. When inside the unit I noticed the other children also had their shirts off (thankfully the mother of the children had her shirt on), but the result was a modification to the thermostat. We installed a lockbox that fits around the thermostat and keeps it at pre-set temperature. This received some complaints and took some adjusting but the heating bill went down by two-thirds to a reasonable amount per month.

I am often asked if renting to section 8 tenants is a profitable decision. The answer depends on the type of agency providing the subsidy. Just in the Chicago area alone, we have contracts with four different subsidy organizations. Three of them are fantastic, but one is awful. The advantage from the landlords perspective is obviously having guaranteed rent. The disadvantage is being at the organization's mercy when it comes to occupancy inspections. I recently had a unit on the South Side of Chicago that was subsidized by the awful organization. When the inspector came out, he wrote several violations that needed to be corrected within thirty days. A few of them were very petty, but we completed everything on the list. We passed their annual occupancy inspection on the second attempt, which was nothing short of a miracle. However, two weeks later, they gave us a random surprise inspection that revealed even more work to do in the basement (the tenant lived on the second floor). This was not the first time this type of behavior has occurred, and it is because the inspectors work for a private, independent company. The more inspections they conduct, the more money they extract from the government. Finally, I had enough and sold the building. The answer is simple; be careful. Find the right tenants, and use only the best organizations. Often the tenants will play you against the organization and make you appear to be negligent. It is crucial you document everything with photographs and witnesses in the case of a dispute. However, if you find the right tenant, it can be a very rewarding and profitable experience.

On another occasion I did a routine inspection of a rental apartment when I found a number of unknown people living in the unit. The lease specifies that only the authorized tenants may reside in the unit, but they had cousins, second cousins, and cousins of the second cousins living there. I felt like an immigration officer discovering people hiding in the attic and closets. Disgraceful, and also an immediate termination of the lease. This is an extreme example, but it highlights the leverage you will have when you only authorize a few people to reside in the unit.

There was a rental unit very close to a college that brought in over $1,000 per month. While it was an excellent income-producing property, it was also an enormous headache. We had rented the unit to two Swedish girls who attended the university. On the conclusion of their semester in December, they left for a few weeks to return to Sweden. Unfortunately for us, they shut off their heat completely. The weather was very cold that year, and as a matter of science, the pipes burst when the water froze. The frozen water actually caused a temporary loss of water to the entire tier of apartments—until the pipe burst. When they returned after the first of the year, they came back to an apartment that resembled more of a swimming pool than a residential unit. Because so many of the tenants in the building were students, the issue was not reported until they came home. She blamed us for the cause of the flooding, claiming that in Sweden they do not have this issue (as if it does not get cold there?). She was hysterical, claiming all of her belongings were ruined, and because she was a student had nowhere else to go and no money for a hotel. She demanded we pay to replace all of her ruined furniture and clothes; she did not even have rental insurance policy of her own (we had suggested she obtain one). The condominium insurance company luckily took responsibility to repair most of the damage to the unit, although we lost two months of rent and had to finish the flooring and paint the new drywall. The lesson here is that young renters are often clueless and take no responsibility for their actions. I was young and dumb once as well, so I understand—but I was never so dumb as to leave my heat off in the middle of winter.

There was a unit on the Northwest Side of Chicago, in an upscale area by O'Hare airport, that seemed like it had good potential as a rental. I noticed the rental amount in the building was over $900 per month and the interior condition was above average, so we obtained a tax deed and kept it as a rental property. I only needed to paint it and install new appliances. I found someone I thought was a good tenant: a professional realtor (who was also a professional waiter). He was educated, well spoken, and needed a new apartment. I spoke with his managing broker, checked his credit, and he moved in. From the start I described it as a night terror—not a nightmare, but the type kids get when they simply wake up screaming for their lives. He was always behind on rent and would only pay (or borrow money) at the last minute to keep his lease in compliance. Worse yet, he was constantly complaining. We fixed an item, but it was never fixed correctly it seemed; he used this as an excuse to avoid paying rent. He was rude and demanding, yet I was even more rude and demanding for my rent. The building was managed professionally but terribly—most of the other owners and renters were miserable, and yet the assessments were high. I am providing some of the comedy—I mean correspondence—from him, as it highlights some of the insanity you will come up against as a landlord. As you will see from the letters, although he initially prefers to terminate his lease, he quickly backs off and is apologetic, blaming his girlfriend. In typical fashion for him and so many other renters, there is a selfishness that prevents them from taking any responsibility for their actions. Before the remorse occurs, they will test the waters to see how far they can push you, and I suggest you know the law well to avoid being sued and to use the proper leverage.

untitled attachment 00443

I have had enough this place is a slum, unsafe and dangerous, and infested with bugs! You can consider this my last month here!

You can use the last month I paid ahead of time, as my rent for this month.

I will do my best to try and be out by the 1st, if I can find something within the next couple weeks.

If I am not able to get out by the 1st, then I will vacate the premises immediately upon securing another residence.

I will keep you informed... As soon as I have another lease signed, you will be notified immediately and I will give you my move out date, which will absolutely be ASAP!!!

He also included this attachment, which was posted all over the apartment building by some of the other owners who were unhappy—this essentially fueled his fire.

ASSOCIATION IS OBLIGATED TO MAINTAIN BUT WE ARE GETTING LOUSY MAINTENACE & TERRIBLE REPSONSE FROM ASSOC. & BLDNG MANAGEMENT!!!

CALL/CONTACT LISA MADIGAN , ILLINOIS ATTORNEY GENERAL, http://illinoisattorneygeneral.gov & YOUR BUILDING BOARD MEMBER,

GO TO YELP TO POST YOUR OPINION.

1. KNIFE ATTACKS ON PROPERTY. ROBBERIES IN BUILDING BUT NO SECURITY STAFF OR CAMERAS.
2. BED BUG INFESTATION.
3. TERRIBLE BUILDING MAINTENANCE CONDITIONS.
4. HALLWAY CARPETS FILTHY, SMELLY, NEVER WASHED & COVERED WITH STAINS.
5. DIRTY HALLWAY WINDOWS.
6. NO AIR CONDITIONING IN COMMON AREAS, LAUNDRY ROOM. MAKES HALLWAYS/BUILDINGS HOT & SMELLY.
7. CHARGING FEES TO USE SWIMMING POOL & VISITOR'S PARKING THAT ARE SUPPOSED TO BE PART OF THE AMENITIES WITH LIVING HERE.
8. ELEVATORS BROKEN FOR DAYS.

MOST OF THE RESIDENTS ARE VERY DIS-SATISFIED WITH MANAGEMENT, HOA/BOARD MEMBERS & BUILDING CONDITIONS.

WE ALL HAVE RIGHTS TO FIGHT AND VOTE FOR NEW, MORE RESPONSIBLE BOARD MEMBERS AND NEW MANAGEMENT CO.

And of course, the apology comes next:

Tim Gray

From:
Sent: Thursday, June 20, 2013 6:04 PM
To: Tim Gray
Subject: Lease

Tim,

I want to apologize for all of the back and fourth concerning the apartment.

The reason I have had so many complaints and issues is because of my now ex girlfriend. She had frequently stayed over and has been complaining and b...... to me about things ever since I moved in and has been pushing me to move.

When she saw the letter posted in the elevator that I sent to you, she freaked out and said I had to move or she wasn't coming back and had refused to stay here since she saw the letter.

So, it was never my intention to give you guys such a hard time, complain, or terminate the lease, but it was what she kept pressuring me to do.

Since I emailed you to terminate the lease, her and I have decided to go our separate ways and are no longer going to be involved in a relationship. We could not meet eye to eye over my living situation here and that didn't sit well with me, especially after the work it took to get this unit; I think all she cared about was her personal interest and not how it effected my life.

With that being said, I would like to respectfully apologize for the hardships I've put fourth to you and your team. There are some issues here with the unit, but nothing that cannot be worked through, the main issue was her.

I know I asked to terminate the lease, but after consideration and the breakup with my girlfriend, I would like to remain in the unit if that is possible.

I can bring you the money for this month including the late fee and can pay you in time, on the 1st of July for next month and every month forward until the end of the term, if you would be willing to allow me to stay in the unit and complete the term of the lease?

Pleas let me know asap if this would be possible.

Thank you,

Real Estate Broker

Safe to say I worked this guy out fast. This story is intended to show the realities of renting. I do agree with his frustration in this case, as the building should not have been managed so poorly. It was somewhat out of our control, as we were only one owner of about one hundred, and were paying high assessments for a building that was not being maintained. There was also the threat of a lawsuit, which I see so often when a renter wants to deflect some blame onto me, even though the issue is with him. All of this was started because he did not pay rent and I began playing hardball. To counter the failure to pay rent, he deflected with threats of litigation and interior condition complaints:

BY THE WAY TIM, I CUT MY FINGER PRETTY BAD ON YOUR SLIDING DOOR THAT BROKE WITH IN A WEEK OF LIVING THERE AND DIDN'T MENTION IT, BUT I THINK I WILL GO AHEAD WITH A LAWSUIT AGAINST YOU INSTEAD, SINCE THIS IS HOW YOU CHOSE TO HANDLE THINGS AS A "REAL ESTATE PROFESSIONAL".

Of course, if someone were actually that unhappy, why would they want to stay there? The answer: they want to live for free. No one knows better than I that free housing can make up for many negative issues in a building, even including lack of electricity and water service. But should a tenant have to actually pay for their residence, some will demand five-star treatment.

He was the last tenant in that unit; I took the advice of the neighbors in that flyer and sold the property, ironically back to the bank who had lost it to taxes in the first place. Not only did I sell it back to the bank that failed to pay the taxes (and assessments) for over three years, but I also collected rent ($900 per month) for an additional year before they even woke up and realized their error. Shockingly, they had sold the note to a third party. This "note" was not theirs to begin with once a tax deed was issued, but they sold it anyway in a package of distressed property to an investor, which highlights the way they conduct their business.

The landlord business can be very rewarding and incredibly frustrating. If done properly, you can achieve excellent results. Without adequate reserves, you can fail easily. A landlord-tenant dispute is sure to arise, so get an insurance policy that will cover you. I prefer everything in writing when there is a dispute.

THE FORECLOSURE CRISIS

THE PERIOD BETWEEN 2005 and 2007 set the stage for the real estate collapse in 2008. Many homeowners and investors took out mortgages for properties that they could barely afford to pay and that were valued far in excess of their worth. Some loans did not even require verification of income, simply signing a statement telling them you made enough to pay the monthly mortgage was sufficient. Since 2008, it has become next to impossible to obtain or refinance a loan, with an application process that requires essentially every answer be in the banks favor—any situation even construed as negative is an automatic rejection. It is this all-or-nothing attitude that has created the real estate downfall. The larger banks take no time to get to know the applicant, they simply see in black and white. You have a slightly better chance to refinance or purchase a principle residence, but long gone are the days of obtaining a mortgage on an investment property. Because they have rejected so many applicants for mortgages since 2008, only investors with cash on hand are able to purchase investment property. This has driven prices down to the floor, as only a few have liquid cash to purchase properties in the latest recession. Many of the banks needed a bail out, which they received from the United States government—or more accurately, the taxpayers of the United States. The very same people whose property has been foreclosed and who have been rejected on applications for new mortgages and refinances are the ones who bailed out these large banks. They used this money to create liquidity, remove their "toxic" assets from their financial statements, and begin anew—with lessons learned and new rejection strategies. The people who paid for this are indeed still paying for it, living paycheck to paycheck with no way to rid themselves of their own toxic assets, and they continue to get bullied by the same banks who are now light on their feet.

One of the ways they have removed themselves from bad loans is simply by not paying the real estate taxes on foreclosed or abandoned property. Rather than use the bail out money to work with (and improve) communities by lending to investors and nonprofit groups or doing mortgage modifications, they simply stop paying the taxes on the home and let it go to a tax sale. Once a tax buyer like me obtains a deed to the property, it comes right off of their books, and they have rid themselves of the toxic asset. Since they have much tax to write off with their profits (monthly fees, overdrawn penalties, and interest rates on good loans), it is essentially a win-win for the big banks. They can rid themselves of the property and use the large write off to avoid paying taxes to the very same government and people who bailed them out in the first place. It is disgraceful—especially because many times they leave the property in ruins. Sometimes they will sell the property to an investor with an active tax lien and the investor will call bewildered as how they could owe years of property tax from before they even purchased this new "investment." Let's look at our first example:

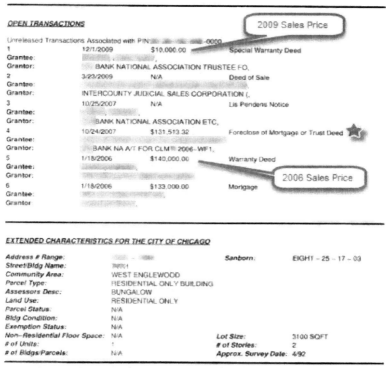

This is a title report from a company called Realinfo LLC. This is a pay service we use, which I highly recommend for the ease of use. However, titles are public records. The transactions are listed from most recent (1) to the oldest entry (6). Report is used with permission.

Let me explain this title report and what happened in this case, which is one of hundreds of thousands nationwide. If you look at the fifth entry you will see the home was sold on January 18, 2006 for $140,000. On the very same day, at the closing, he took out a mortgage for $133,000, putting only $7,000 down (or 5 percent). Approximately sixteen months later the lender began foreclosure proceedings on him, foreclosing on $131,513. So in a year and a half, he failed to make the monthly payments and only paid down less than $2,000 of the mortgage. If you look at entry two, you will see it took approximately two years, until March 23, 2009, before the home was offered at a foreclosure sale. Even though it appears it was sold at the foreclosure sale, it was not sold at all. There was no winning bidder. The lender had sold this in a package deal to a bank in a portfolio (consisting mostly of distressed property). Since there was no bidder for this home, the bank hired a realtor to sell it on the open market through the MLS. And as evidenced by entry 1—on December 1, 2009, it was sold for only $10,000. You can bet the bank took a loss and also a tax write off of the same amount that year. I discovered this when it was offered in the Cook County tax sale for the 2008 taxes in 2010. The new owner did not pay the real estate taxes, nor did the bank as they exited stage right. I did not place a bid on it. As I write this, I just looked up the delinquent tax situation. There are now six straight years of unpaid taxes on this home. The new owner did not pay a single installment of tax—I guess paying $10,000 was enough for him—and no tax buyer felt like purchasing the tax lien on a home worth only $10,000. Cook County was the big loser.

Want more?

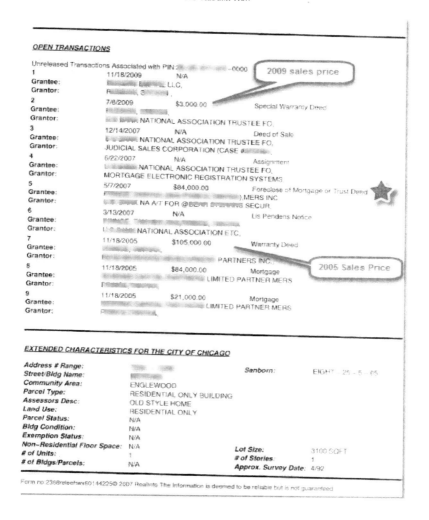

OPEN TRANSACTIONS

Unreleased Transactions Associated with PIN: ▓▓ ▓▓ ▓▓ ▓▓ -0000

1	11/18/2009	N/A	2009 sales price
Grantee:	▓▓▓▓▓ ▓▓▓▓▓ LLC,		
Grantor:	R▓▓▓▓, S▓▓▓▓,		
2	7/8/2009	$3,000.00	Special Warranty Deed
Grantee:	▓▓▓▓▓, ▓▓▓▓▓,		
Grantor:	▓▓▓ ▓▓▓ NATIONAL ASSOCIATION TRUSTEE FO,		
3	12/14/2007	N/A	Deed of Sale
Grantee:	▓ ▓ ▓▓▓ NATIONAL ASSOCIATION TRUSTEE FO,		
Grantor:	JUDICIAL SALES CORPORATION (CASE #▓▓▓▓▓		
4	6/22/2007	N/A	Assignment
Grantee:	▓ ▓▓▓▓ NATIONAL ASSOCIATION TRUSTEE FO,		
Grantor:	MORTGAGE ELECTRONIC REGISTRATION SYSTEMS		
5	5/7/2007	$84,000.00	Foreclose of Mortgage or Trust Deed
Grantee:	▓▓▓▓▓ ▓▓▓▓▓ ▓▓▓▓▓ ▓▓▓▓▓ ▓▓▓▓▓),MERS INC		
Grantor:	▓▓ ▓▓▓▓ NA A/T FOR @▓▓▓▓ ▓▓▓▓▓▓▓ SECUR,		
6	3/13/2007	N/A	Lis Pendens Notice
Grantee:	▓▓▓▓▓ ▓▓▓▓▓ ▓▓▓▓▓, ▓▓▓▓▓		
Grantor:	▓▓ ▓▓▓▓ NATIONAL ASSOCIATION ETC,		
7	11/18/2005	$105,000.00	Warranty Deed
Grantee:	▓▓▓▓▓, ▓▓▓▓▓,		
Grantor:	▓▓▓▓▓ ▓▓▓▓▓ ▓▓▓▓▓ PARTNERS INC,	2005 Sales Price	
8	11/18/2005	$84,000.00	Mortgage
Grantee:	▓▓▓▓▓ ▓▓▓ ▓▓▓▓ LIMITED PARTNER MERS		
Grantor:	▓▓▓▓▓, ▓▓▓▓▓,		
9	11/18/2005	$21,000.00	Mortgage
Grantee:	▓▓▓▓▓ ▓▓▓▓▓ ▓▓▓▓ LIMITED PARTNER MERS		
Grantor:	▓▓▓▓▓▓▓▓,		

EXTENDED CHARACTERISTICS FOR THE CITY OF CHICAGO

Address # Range:	▓▓▓ - ▓▓▓	Sanborn:	EIGHT - 25 - 5 - 05
Street/Bldg Name:	▓▓▓▓▓▓▓		
Community Area:	ENGLEWOOD		
Parcel Type:	RESIDENTIAL ONLY BUILDING		
Assessors Desc:	OLD STYLE HOME		
Land Use:	RESIDENTIAL ONLY		
Parcel Status:	N/A		
Bldg Condition:	N/A		
Exemption Status:	N/A		
Non-Residential Floor Space:	N/A	Lot Size:	3100 SQFT
# of Units:	1	# of Stories:	1
# of Bldgs/Parcels:	N/A	Approx. Survey Date:	4/92

Form no: 2368releehwx601442250 2007 Realinto The information is deemed to be reliable but is not guaranteed

Here we have a home located on the south side of Chicago. On November 18, 2005 this property was sold for $105,000. A mortgage was taken out at closing for the exact same amount, meaning it was sold with no money down. On March 13, 2007 foreclosure proceedings were filed, and on December 14 of that year it was offered at the foreclosure sale, but no one placed a bid on the property. You will see the word "trustee" listed next to an entry, as they simply helped liquidate this home from a lender who is no longer around. The trustee sold the property on July 8, 2009 for only $3,000. The individual who purchased it got a great deal; but also repaired the home, redeemed the tax sale, and took out a new mortgage in 2011. This is a good example of how a savvy investor can be patient and buy at the right time. It is also a reminder of the perils of the no money down strategy and not having enough adequate money in savings to be able to pay for what you borrow.

Below are two more examples of the same type of insanity. The first example originally sold for $255,000, with no money down, and eventually sold for only $14,500, complete with a water lien to pay off as well. The second example was sold for $228,000 and once foreclosure proceedings were through—the market crashed; the home wrecked and abused—it sold for only $36,000. When you add up the losses from only the examples I have provided, it totals almost $1 million. Sadly, these are only a handful of examples of a nationwide crisis that we as taxpayers helped to both create and resolve. All of the buyers who were foreclosed purchased with the best of intentions; and all of the investors who picked at the bones profited from their failure—as well as that of the banks.

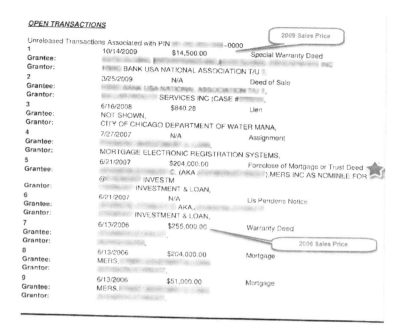

OPEN TRANSACTIONS

Unreleased Transactions Associated with PIN ▓▓ ▓▓ ▓▓ ▓▓▓-0000

2009 Sales Price

1	10/14/2009	$14,500.00	Special Warranty Deed

Grantee: ▓▓▓▓ ▓▓▓▓ ▓▓▓▓▓▓▓▓▓▓ ▓▓ ▓▓ ▓▓▓ ▓▓▓▓▓▓▓ ▓▓▓▓ INC
Grantor: ▓▓▓▓ BANK USA NATIONAL ASSOCIATION T/U ▓

2	3/25/2009	N/A	Deed of Sale

Grantee: ▓▓▓ BANK USA NATIONAL ASSOCIATION T/U ▓,
Grantor: ▓▓▓ ▓▓▓▓▓▓▓ SERVICES INC (CASE #▓▓▓▓▓▓,

3	6/16/2008	$840.28	Lien

Grantee: NOT SHOWN,
Grantor: CITY OF CHICAGO DEPARTMENT OF WATER MANA,

4	7/27/2007	N/A	Assignment

Grantee: ▓▓▓▓▓▓ ▓▓▓▓▓▓▓ ▓ ▓▓▓▓,
Grantor: MORTGAGE ELECTRONIC REGISTRATION SYSTEMS,

5	6/21/2007	$204,000.00	Foreclose of Mortgage or Trust Deed ⭐

Grantee: ▓▓▓▓▓▓▓ ▓▓▓▓▓▓▓ C. (AKA ▓▓▓▓▓▓▓ ▓▓▓▓▓),MERS INC AS NOMINEE FOR
@▓▓▓▓▓▓ INVESTM
Grantor: ▓▓▓▓▓▓ INVESTMENT & LOAN,

6	6/21/2007	N/A	Lis Pendens Notice

Grantee: ▓▓▓▓▓ ▓▓▓▓▓▓ ▓ AKA, ▓▓▓▓▓▓▓ ▓▓▓▓▓▓
Grantor: ▓▓▓▓▓▓ INVESTMENT & LOAN,

7	6/13/2006	$255,000.00	Warranty Deed

Grantee: ▓▓▓▓▓▓▓▓▓▓▓
Grantor: ▓▓▓▓▓▓▓▓▓,

2006 Sales Price

8	6/13/2006	$204,000.00	Mortgage

Grantee: MERS, ▓▓▓▓▓ ▓▓▓▓▓▓▓ ▓▓▓▓▓▓▓
Grantor: ▓▓▓▓▓▓▓▓ ▓▓▓▓▓,

9	6/13/2006	$51,000.00	Mortgage

Grantee: MERS, ▓▓▓▓▓ ▓▓▓▓▓▓▓▓▓
Grantor: ▓▓▓▓▓▓▓▓▓ ▓▓▓▓▓,

EXTENDED CHARACTERISTICS FOR THE CITY OF CHICAGO

Address # Range:	▓▓▓▓ ▓▓▓▓		
Street/Bldg Name:	GREEN	Sanborn:	EIGHT – 25 – 21 – 03
Community Area:	ENGLEWOOD		
Parcel Type:	RESIDENTIAL ONLY BUILDING		
Assessors Desc:	TWO & FOUR FLATS – BRICK		
Land Use:	RESIDENTIAL ONLY		
Parcel Status:	N/A		
Bldg Condition:	N/A		
Exemption Status:	N/A		
Non–Residential Floor Space:	N/A		
# of Units:	2	Lot Size:	3000 SQFT
# of Bldgs/Parcels:	N/A	# of Stories:	2
		Approx. Survey Date:	4/92

Form no.2191releehwx1012415269 2007 RealInfo The Information is deemed to be reliable but is not guaranteed.

Below we have a property that sold for the price of only $1. That's right, this home for only a buck. If you notice at the bottom, the listing mandates that you do not sell the property within sixty days of the purchase. This is known as a deed restriction, only used by the big banks, to minimize their embarrassment when you sell for double (in this case it would be $2) or more. Notice the compensation: $1,250 to the agent who brings in the buyer, plus the listing agent gets paid as well. I repeat, $1,250 in commission for a home that sold for a dollar. What business in the world could keep their doors open with such a ridiculous business model? I would be living by the railroad tracks if I ran my business this way, but unlike this bank, I do not have the ability to get bailed out or insure my losses with the government.

Keep in mind that at one time there was a large mortgage on this, plus it was a two-unit building. That is only fifty cents per unit. The losses add up to figures that would make anyone's head spin. If you think that last example was irresponsible (and who wouldn't), then strap on your seatbelt.

Recently we had a tax lien that had expired; no redemption was made. I checked the MLS and noticed the property was listed for sale. It was owned by a large international bank and was listed as a short sale. I asked the agent about it, and whether the bank wanted to simply pay off the tax lien directly to us, thinking maybe they had missed the date by accident. How wrong I was: as it turned out, they knew all along they were responsible for those three years of taxes and refused to pay it unless they found a buyer. They hired an attorney who had been working on the short sale the entire time and tried to get them to redeem the taxes before they lost it. This bank obviously had the $8,000 to pay the taxes, but they would rather waste the realtor's time, an attorney's time who represented them, and a prospective buyer who didn't offer enough money to make it worthwhile. I called and spoke with the attorney and told her how disgusted I was with the bank; they owned the property over those last three years and should pay the tax they owe. She agreed. I contacted the agent again and asked her to bring forth anyone who offered anything, so maybe I could finally get her paid by doing a direct sale. I can't show her name, but I will write the words she wrote for you to see:

"The bank is awful—I really don't feel they want to help with the housing foreclosure issues....but that's another conversation. I will also forward the email with the offer. Have a great day."

So this chapter is well named: some banks have caused and prolonged the foreclosure crisis, keeping the values down (selling for a dollar), and simply not caring about anything but themselves. Yet, those banks are only around because *you* give them money to deposit, *you* borrow money from them—and pay it back with interest. *You* bailed them out.

THE AUCTIONS

I HAVE BEEN AN auctioneer for more than twelve years, and becoming one was the single best decision of my life. Besides learning a great auction chant and having the ability to raise money at charity events, it has made me into a better bidder at auctions. Learning to sell has made me a better buyer. I have sold hundreds of properties ranging in price from $10,000 to more than $1,000,000. There is no difference in my style or my cadence, the price is just a number—and the number is just a sales price. From the buyers' standpoint a $2 million home that sells for $1 million is just as good of a deal as a $20,000 home that sells for $10,000. In mathematical theory, of course. On the flip side, I have sold property to some bidders who have the fever—or the ego—and are not willing to lose. I remember attending an auction as a buyer and getting outbid on a condo by at least $50,000 (it sold for over $200,000); I felt the buyer (and the other buyers who took him to that price) were out of their minds. I was hired to be an auctioneer a few months later and as luck would have it, that very same buyer was bidding. Before the auction I started a conversation with him and asked him if he had viewed the property he bid so aggressively on a few months earlier. He was stoic, telling me no, he hadn't, but that he didn't care. But I had visited the property, and the place was a complete disaster, totally outdated from the 60s with junk everywhere. It was in a high-rise building on the far North Side of Chicago, and I have learned those clean outs are expensive and a pain. You need to pay for elevator time, there is no place to bring and store a dumpster. It was only one-bedroom, yet he paid the price of a totally remodeled two-bedroom unit. He shrugged his shoulders and was somewhat indignant. He was much more reserved at the auction I was conducting, but only because there was no one there to put him on the spot and make him feel feverish or insecure.

I have also conducted auctions with a main level and a balcony level, getting bids from both floors and feeling the excitement of the room. From the perspective of the auctioneer, nothing is more exciting, and the same is true from the buyers' perspective. It is part real estate sale, part rock-and-roll show. No one likes to lose, and yet auctions are not about winning and losing, they are about investing. My attitude as a bidder is simple: when the bidding goes far past my target price, "Let him have it." I don't take it personally and do not get emotional over the process, and this is valuable advice. It is your money; spend it wisely. Set a target price and stick to it, perhaps increase it at the sale by 10 percent or less if you feel the other bidder is coming close to their final bid. You will see them take their time and stammer a bit, and you know they are close to their breaking point. Take him high enough so that when you are done, he regrets having gone so high. At one scavenger sale I remember getting into a bidding war and actually saying out loud, "It's yours," when I stopped bidding. He was declared the winner and within thirty seconds I could hear him talking to himself. He was mad at himself and even more mad at me, as if I played some type of mind trick on him, taking him on a rollercoaster bidding ride and leaving him at the top, all alone.

At the same time, if you miss out on a property for only a thousand dollars, it can be a very long ride home. You can't control the other bidder; the only thing you can control is yourself. Always view the property, know what you are bidding on and stick to your game plan.

Auctioneers are a hardworking, entrepreneurial group. Unlike others who like to work for a brokerage, auctioneers tend to work by themselves, and they work hard. Most of all, I have learned that ethics and moral values are the most important part of being a successful auctioneer. Having a fantastic auction chant does not hurt either. If the audience does not trust you, it does not matter what you are selling—they will not buy it. This differs from realtors and attorneys who struggle to gain trust. As an auctioneer you can offer Elvis Presley's first guitar for sale, but if the audience doesn't trust you (and thinks it may be a fake), no one will bid. The same applies to shady bidders, if you get a reputation as someone who bids but does not pay, you will become infamous—fast. Neither last long in the industry.

One of the greatest compliments I have ever received came at the conclusion of a charity auction. The charity was very worthwhile, and I felt fortunate to help raise a lot of money during the live auction that night. One of the benefactors of the charity came to me and told me how much he enjoyed the way I conducted myself: "I have no money, but you made me want to bid."

One memory that stands out involves an auction to a packed house. The real estate market was at the top and the bidding was very active. This was one of my earlier auctions, and it was made much easier by the attendance of a basketball legend. While his incredible accomplishments on the court had recently come to a conclusion, his new life was focused on real estate investing. He was part bidder, part celebrity—and he kept the action moving at the same fast pace he played basketball. He was an aggressive bidder but not foolish, getting the action started quickly, sometimes bidding in increments higher than I was even requesting. Once the price had gone past his targeted amount he politely backed out, but by then he had created a wave of bidding activity that was easy for me to carry forward. He purchased a number of properties that day, but the ones he did not purchase he helped me sell by getting the excitement going. He either flipped or rented the properties, a good strategy for him, since any prospective renter was thrilled to have a basketball legend as a landlord. When he did flip the property, he included an autographed basketball as a closing gift, a touch of class—but also a great sales technique.

Once the economy crashed, conducting an auction was more painful than extracting wisdom teeth without Novocain. I worked a number of auctions that did not go well. Compared to my competition I was still successfully selling, although the prices had dropped considerably. Buyers no longer wanted to get into bidding wars; they wanted to be assured they were getting a great deal. The only way to do this was to start with lower opening bids, which made the sellers nervous. If your seller needs $100,000 and you start with $1, you have a ton of ground to make up in order to complete a sale. If you start at $75,000, no one will show up. It was tough to find the middle ground. One auction involved a high-rise condominium unit that a younger man and his mother were attempting to sell. They chose a low opening bid and an absolute auction to attract more buyers (*absolute* means it will sell regardless of price). This made me nervous for them, but the auction company did a fine job of explaining the terms, and I felt they understood the process. The bidding was slow, I am not sure I've ever worked harder in my life to sell a property. I knew the price they aspired to achieve, as well as the price that would have been acceptable. I had to pull a few tongue twisters out—some time-stalling mechanisms, telling bidders to "take their time" and "going once, going twice, going two-and-a-half times. Did I see an eyebrow raise sir?" "Don't worry sir, we have the room until midnight" "Do you want to call your wife sir? We will wait!" When the gavel finally fell and it was sold, I felt we obtained the highest price we could, which was over the price we had expected to sell for, but less than what they aspired to. This was at the bottom of the market, and it was tough. After the auction, I was exhausted and before leaving said good-bye to the young man and his mom. I was expecting a thank you or some gratitude for my effort—which I was proud of, but instead he said to me: "You just threw away my inheritance. How can you possibly think you did a good job?" Perhaps he was under the impression that auctioneers are magicians, but he was lucky to get the price he did. I do not think they ever closed on the unit, refusing to sign the closing documents, and frankly they were lucky the buyer didn't sue them and the auction company.

There are many different types of auctions. The tax lien auction in Illinois for example is unique because only the interest rate is the subject of the bidding. You are only bidding on the interest to be received when the owner redeems the tax sale.

You can't bid lower than 0 percent (which is where most of the bidding occurs), so the auctioneer must determine which of the 0 percent bidders to choose. This is no easy task when the entire room is screaming "zero" at the same time, as loud as possible, eight hours a day. Buyers would take creative measures to capture the auctioneer's attention. Some would make creative signs, while others would wear bright clothing. Some buyers hired attractive women to bid, which was a very effective strategy for the male auctioneer, but seemed to backfire when female auctioneers took the gavel. Above all else, the seating placement in the bidding room was far and away the single most important ingredient to a successful tax sale. It doesn't matter how fast a bidder you are or how good you look, you must be seen by the auctioneer. This makes the front row of a tax sale room prime real estate. The treasurer will usually draw names from a hat, and once your name is called you may sit anywhere that is available. At the Cook County tax sale, I almost always got a front row seat. This is an amazing accomplishment considering the time period of well over a decade. It wasn't just luck of the Irish, a bit of it was timing as well. The treasurer would draw names every Monday at 8:00 a.m. and once you selected your seat it was reserved for the remainder of the week. Some buyers were anxious and lined up early, getting the first available tickets. I had it timed to the minute—the last minute—and often took the last ticket. Of course, the last ticket is also often the first on top of the pile, and my name was among the first to be called on the vast majority of occasions.

Over the last few years the tax sale auction in Illinois has become automated, which has benefited my business as a computer, rather than a human, randomly determines the 0 percent bidder when multiple bids are presented. The auction is now a blind bidding format, which has also helped greatly. My blood pressure used to rise when someone sitting in the back of the room (that clearly did not do any homework) raised their hand and bid—only because I raised mine. There are only a dozen or so companies sophisticated enough to know what they are bidding on, and amateurs benefitted from my homework. The auctioneer for the county (who was not actually a professionally trained or licensed auctioneer) would spread the bidding around the room and actually call on those amateur players sometimes. But no longer. Now that the bids are sealed, everyone must do their own research before bidding. The treasurer, for example, only publishes the amount delinquent for that one year's tax sale. There is no mention of possibly twenty years of back tax that may come with the property, let alone the property may be fire damaged or demolished. There are countless scenarios of financial devastation waiting for you at the tax lien auction. At one mortgage foreclosure sale, I saw a bidder place a bid of over $100,000 on a property, having no idea there was a second mortgage taken out for $90,000 that needed to be paid, plus a tax lien in the amount of $15,000. His face turned a shade of grey I had never seen before when a competitor jovially told him the news. I thought he might need a defibrillator.

There are more traditional types of auctions held for real estate, including absolute and reserve price auctions. An absolute auction, as mentioned, can be a rewarding experience; the seller must accept the highest bid that day, regardless of price. Should it snow that morning or if there is an accident on the expressway, you may have an excellent chance of getting the item at an outstanding price. Whereas at a "reserve price" auction, you can be the only bidder in the room, but if your bid does not meet the seller's "reserve," they are under no obligation to sell. Both approaches have their positives and negatives, but studies have consistently shown that absolute auctions bring in the highest prices. While you may think they would yield the best deals, they tend to bring out the largest number of bidders and therefore drive the prices higher. Some sellers will allow you to purchase the property before the auction occurs, similar to eBay's "buy it now" feature, while others prefer to wait to see the fever spread. No matter the format, read the fine print. Know everything about the type of auction being conducted, and ask questions prior to the auction if needed. There may be a "buyer's premium," which is essentially a commission added to your bid, usually ranging between 5 and 10 percent. This is the cost of running the auction, placed on you, the bidder. While I do not support this personally, if there is a buyer's premium at the auction, you must simply factor it to your purchase price. It is similar to sales tax: for example, a store may advertise *that jacket is 25 percent off!* The price was $100 but now it is *25 percent off!* But they never mention that tax is around 10 to12 percent, so that $75 jacket is actually more than $82. Most bidders neglect this, and it has a bite if you overbid. If there is only one jacket left in the store, but four people want it; the price is $75, but one may take it at $85, another at $95, and the fourth will pay $105, because, damn it, I *want* that jacket. That is a total sales price of $115. And that is the essence of an auction and the beginning of buyer's remorse. Yes, you got the jacket you wanted, but you should be aware the world is not running out of jackets any time soon.

Never attend an auction looking like a million dollars; wear the worst clothes you can. Do not talk to anyone at the auction; you could be accused of bid rigging. Politely decline any conversation with other bidders. Do not leave any notes or books open. If you go to the bathroom, take your materials; I learned this lesson the hard way and came back to find someone scrolling through my notebook. Before the auction starts, listen instead of talking to hear what others are saying. Order a title report or view the recorder of deeds online website or do a freedom of information search. If you are unable to gain interior access to the property before the auction, try to talk to neighbors, do building violation searches, and check the garage out (the garage is always the most neglected item in the home, and can be a good indication on what to expect inside). But always assume the worst. Leave room for the unknown in your pricing, and remember to expect the unexpected.

Raising money for charity.

CLOSING CEREMONIES

IN CLOSING I want to share a strategy I have developed through years of buying and selling. I am not sure how I developed this method, since I am a positive and honest person. Perhaps it was from others using this technique, or possibly it is from figuring out how the world spins around me. Or maybe I am just getting good at this. This technique works best when you want to buy something, but it does work when selling as well. The biggest mistake you can make when buying something is to show the seller you are interested, or worse that you *love* it. Often a couple will walk through a home, and the wife might show her emotional connection and love for the kitchen or bath or the husband will marvel over the garage or basement. "This place is perfect" or "I love this kitchen!" Those are possibly the worst words you can say. You'll want to act as if you hate what is being offered; that it is outdated and overpriced, and they should be embarrassed to even present it. I used this strategy when buying my last car. I told the salesman I was disgusted, shocked in fact, that after all these years of wanting a car like this that there was such a poor example of quality on display. He was bewildered, not knowing what to say. Almost confused, he finally said, "Well sir, we are all about the experience," "Well this experience is a total disappointment," I responded. I explained I was on my way back to my old dealer, since they have better pricing, more technology, and actually know how to treat their customers (which is all true). I received a call from the general manager the next day, who was legitimately upset. I explained what I had said the day before, and although I was completely disgusted with the vehicle, I remained incredibly interested in it. He offered a chance to make it up to me, and sent me an online quote that was far lower than what I would have obtained if I had shown my love and excitement for the new car. I called him back, "You call this a good deal?—Yeah—well then I'll take it." And I drove away happily ever after. The same should be applied to buying a home: the roof, foundation, mechanicals, the comparable sales in the area—all of the negatives should be your leverage. Turn the positives around—a great location can be a nightmare for parking! Never seem happy until the moving truck is pulling up to move your stuff inside. When you are selling, use the opposite approach, seem insulted anyone could find the home too small, overpriced, and outdated. The home is "quaint," "priced to sell," and "vintage!"

I have learned everyone has to live somewhere—unless they want to be homeless, and the streets, especially in Chicago are not comfortable. I rented an apartment to a nice family who at one time lived under a bridge in California. He told a very sad tale of immigration and years of poverty. He wasn't addicted to anything and was a very hard worker. It was a privilege to provide him an apartment in Chicago; he had found work here and was an excellent tenant. His children were well spoken and sweet, and I am sure those days under the bridge will never be forgotten. Of course, at one point he did stop paying rent, was issued a five-day notice, and vanished into thin air. These stories are reminders of the extreme nature of this world, and why we must treat each other with compassion. Unfortunately, no good deed goes unpunished, as the saying goes, and those who offer generosity open themselves up to being taken advantage of. Personally I find this a small price to pay; the reward is helping those who appreciate it. My thank-you comes internally, knowing I have made a difference and will continue to do so.

Having suffered a bad car accident and near death experience, I know how abruptly life can end. I was coming home on May 13, 2001 in a taxicab, when we were struck at high speed by a car exiting an expressway. In the corner of my eye, just a moment before impact, I saw lights at eye level and knew what was coming. Within only a matter of a split-second I had answered a question to which I had asked myself growing up, almost obsessively. "Aha, so this is how I die." But thankfully, I woke up in the middle of the street when a firefighter with a large rubber glove picked me up by the back of the neck, assuming I was dead. That was the start of my new life, one that has been filled with hard work and worry, but without fear of descending backward. The clock is always ticking, sometimes in circular patterns, but always forward. Life is about improving, a process that never ends. My advice is to pick something (anything) and enjoy getting really, really good at it. In my case, I have become an expert at buying tax liens, one of the roads less traveled in the real estate industry. It has been quite a long and enlightening journey. I enjoy sharing the information I have obtained because without passing it on, it stays with me. I encourage you to do the same, keep a journal or handbook. Track goals and make projections as you would in any boardroom. Reward yourself when you overachieve, and take responsibility when you do not perform. My father was the most important figure in my life, and I remember almost everything he said and did for me. If you are lucky enough to have children, do the same; pass it forward onto them. Like me, they will never forget. I wonder; would he be proud of my endurance, tenaciousness, and my success? And in that moment I know that is one question that needs no answer.

CPSIA information can be obtained at www.ICGtesting.com
Printed in the USA
LVOW10s2157180216

475719LV00028B/125/P